EMMA'S JOURNEY

Sue Forrester

[illegible]

1st April 2002

No. ATRA.

FM

First published in Australia in 2001 by
Bill Molyneux and Sue Forrester
Phone + 61 3 5965 2011
Facsimile + 61 3 5965 2033
www.emmasjourney.com
emma@emmasjourney.com

BLOOMINGS BOOKS

Distributed in Australia by Bloomings Books
Phone + 61 3 9818 6363
Facsimile + 61 3 9818 1862

Molyneux, Bill
Emma's journey : spirits of the high country.

ISBN 1 876473 35 5

1. Airedale terriers - Juvenile fiction. 2. Dogs - Juvenile fiction. 3. Pets death - Juvenile fiction I. Forrester, Susan Glen. II. Dingwall, Jane. III Title

A823.4

Designed, typeset and produced in Australia by
Allan Cornwell

Printed in Australia by First Impressions

EMMA'S JOURNEY

Spirits of the High Country

Bill Molyneux and Sue Forrester

Illustrated by Jane Dingwall

FM

The high wild country

AARON AND EMMA

Aaron was an Airedale Terrier, a fluffy, roly-poly black puppy, with faint gold markings on the edges of his ears. He had a gold patch of fur around his bottom, and a little gold mark on his chest.

When he was eight weeks old, he went to live with Sue and Bill. They lived in the country, in a comfortable house with mud-brick walls and big windows, and a verandah all around it. The house overlooked a billabong, where ducks and swamphens made their homes, and came up to the house each morning and evening for some extra food. Big trees shaded the house, and the verandahs were covered with creepers, which made them cool in summer.

Aaron had his own special bed in the big living room, and he loved to look out through the windows, especially on bright moonlit nights, when he would watch the silver water of the billabong and listen to the quiet sounds of the birds as they called to each other.

Sue and Bill also had a plant nursery, so from his very first day with his new family, Aaron went to work. He loved to waddle around with Sue as she put labels in the plants. She soon discovered that yellow was his favourite colour, when he pulled all the yellow labels out of the pots. Sometimes he would bite off yellow flowers and carry them to Sue in his mouth. She was never cross with him. He

Aaron would bite off the yellow flowers and carry them to Sue ...

loved the way she always laughed softly and picked him up for a cuddle. 'Thank you darling,' she would always say.

He liked all the people who came to the nursery to buy their plants. And he especially liked babies. Sometimes he would get into trouble for licking them in their prams. But mostly people were very understanding.

He grew quickly, and learned about many things. In particular, he learned about going bush. Often Sue and Bill took him for walks in the wooded hills behind their home in the valley, and he learned to recognise the smells of wombats and kangaroos and echidnas in the forest.

His favourite place was the very high wild country. The very first time they took him there, his spirit stirred, as if memories of ancestral moorlands still lived in him. He felt so connected to the broad windswept heathlands and swift creeks, and longed to run free through the flower meadows. Little pathways led through gnarled old snow gums, beckoning him; rocky outcrops and sheltering caves invited him to explore; he could wade in the clear pools and lie on the soft springy grass to rest in the warm sun, with Sue and Bill sitting nearby quietly talking with him. They too loved this country deeply.

Aaron had his first birthday. A couple of days later, Bill found Emma. She was an Airedale just like Aaron, but she was lost and tired and hungry. She was also very woolly and dirty, with tar matted through her coat.

Nobody knew where she had come from or where she belonged, so Bill took her home. Sue and Aaron fell in love with her at first sight. 'What's your name? Where did you come from? Are you going to stay with us?' he asked. His enthusiasm was overwhelming.

Hesitantly she responded. 'I'm Emma . . . I ran away from home.'

'Ran away! What for?'

'I didn't think anybody loved me . . . I was never allowed inside with the family. I was always hungry and I even tried to catch rabbits sometimes. I never got one though.'

Aaron was stunned. He knew only love and comfort. And though he would never admit it, he had plenty to eat.

Sue and Bill gave Emma a big dinner. The next day they gave her a bath and a haircut. She was so obviously neglected, they decided they would not search very hard for her previous owners. Already they loved her dearly, and Aaron was overjoyed to have a mate.

She was a beautiful girl. Her deep brown eyes took on a sparkle, and her blonde and silver curls gleamed with regular brushing. Often she would come back to her new family after a rollicking game with Aaron, her pink tongue panting and her tail wagging hard. Her teeth, though white, were worn down in the front.

She was a beautiful girl ...

'She certainly didn't get calcium when she was a baby,' said Bill, and Sue agreed.

As the days and months rolled by, Aaron and Emma became inseparable. They shared a thousand adventures. If Aaron didn't have a leg in plaster, Emma had echidna quills sticking in her face. Or they would both go wading down the creek, and come home muddy from nose to tail, panting and happy. Sue always gave them a bath then, and sometimes even growled at them, but it was worth it.

Feral cats disappeared fast. But the hundreds of waterbirds that lived on the billabong at home were never disturbed. Just for fun, though, the pair used to chase away the big black ravens who regularly raided the compost heap for scraps, and sometimes went a bit too close to the Airedales' big bones which Sue gave them every day.

The biggest drama occurred one summer. It was nearly fatal. A huge tiger snake came onto the verandah and both Airedales leapt at it. Emma was bitten around the face and neck several times. For a week she hung between life and death, with Sue and Bill taking turns to sit with her each day at the vet hospital, and Aaron visiting often to talk with her in their special language.

It was a year before she was strong enough to walk more than a few hundred metres. That summer, they all went back to the high wild country. Like Aaron, Emma knew this was her special place. The two of them would run for miles, sniffing the scent of hares, wading in the streams, and glorying in the freedom and space of this land. Always they came back to where Sue and Bill were wandering through the flower meadows, and together the four would lie in the dappled shade of the old snow gums, breathing the sweet cool air and listening to the silence of the wild plains.

There was one trip, some time later, when Aaron felt uneasy. Something was not right with Emma. She was lying on her side, eyes closed.

'You don't seem yourself lately, Emma, not your usual bouncy self, anyway,' he said.

She looked up into the handsome worried face that she loved so much. 'I didn't want to worry you,' she said, 'but I've been having such bad pains behind my eyes. When the sun is bright it's even worse.'

He could see the pain in the deep brown eyes, and fear entered his heart.

'I know Sue's going to take us for our needles soon. The doctor will have a good look at you then, I'm sure.'

The vet did his usual thorough check of both Airedales, with Sue standing by their heads. They both noticed Emma's flinching reaction to the light as he looked into each of her eyes.

An x-ray was taken, and it revealed a tumour behind the eye. It spread very quickly. Emma now spent most of her time having treatment at a special hospital, or lying on her bed at home recovering from the treatment. The pain was still very bad, and Aaron was constantly nearby. He knew she was very sick.

'Don't talk if you don't feel like it, Em. I'll just sit with you,' he murmured.

'Thank you,' she whispered. 'Just talk to me about some of the things we've done, and the places we've been with Sue and Bill.'

He lay down beside her as she rested

on her bed, and quietly talked, going back over the seven years they had shared. Often she wouldn't hear him after a while, because she had drifted into a deep sleep. But he just kept talking in his quiet gentle voice.

One mid-summer morning, Sue and Bill carried Emma outside to the deck overlooking the billabong. She rested her head on Sue's lap.

'I feel sleepy so often, now, Aaron. My mind is not here most of the time,' she said.

'Where are you thinking about?' he asked.

'The — the high wild country . . . I know I'm lying here with you and Sue and Bill, but another part of me is up there.'

Images kept flashing into her mind of high windswept heathlands with streams winding across the plains, and patches of snow still lying on the protected sides of rocky outcrops. She had known that this was her spirit home the first time she ever set foot upon it. She sensed it, smelt it, and when she ran freely over it with Aaron beside her, her spirit soared, her sense of final place became fixed, and she knew that some day she would return there forever.

She knew that time was close. Through her clouded eyes, she let her gaze wander over the billabong around which she had run so very many times, and in whose shallows she had buried bones 'for later'. Her concentration became focused on the whirling diving patterns of a flock of swallows, feeding on insects near the surface of the water.

As he listened to Emma, Aaron was watching the swallows too. One in particular caught his eye. It was different from the others. It was pure white.

He could not take his gaze from it as it detached itself from the flock. It flew straight towards them, and swept in a broad circle over Emma. Sue and Bill were watching it too, wondering.

Down it swooped again, and Emma followed it with her eyes. She felt a deep calm come over her, and everything else around her began to recede.

Then she heard it calling. 'Let go, Emma, let go . . . and come with me.'

'Who are you?' she heard herself ask.

'I'm your spirit swallow. I'm here to take you to the high wild country. Your time is very near.'

Again the white swallow circled, swooping up and down in long slow loops.

... the two of them would run for miles ...

'Goodbye white swallow, and thank you … you knew just where I wanted to come ...'

'Just let go, Emma, and come with me; it is time to go.'

As the white swallow swept skywards, Emma felt a slight tug as she left her body to follow. She didn't want to lose the little bird in the wide sky, but she looked back momentarily at the scene below. There were Sue and Bill cradling her still form in their arms, and Aaron was kissing her nose in farewell. Then, as if drawn by a magic thread, she turned and followed the white swallow.

Aaron got up from where he had been sitting and gently sniffed Emma's nose. Sue and Bill wept as they held her warm soft body in their arms, her eyes opal-clear and free from pain at last.

'She's gone,' said Bill. 'She just relaxed and stopped breathing.'

Again Aaron touched his nose to hers. 'Goodbye for now, Emma. I'm glad you're no longer in pain … but I'll miss you terribly,' he murmured quietly into her soft ear.

And then he returned to his own place, and lay down with his chin resting on his paws.

'I know you're going to somewhere beautiful, and we'll be together again some day, but oh how I'll miss you till then.' His heart ached with a great sadness.

They buried Emma on a rise overlooking the billabong. It was evening, and as the sun faded, flocks of birds winged their way to night roosting spots. Bill and Sue and Aaron knew that life would not be the same again without her, and their grief was very heavy.

'Goodbye for now, darling girl,' said Sue.

Yes, for now, thought Aaron. We'll be together again one day.

He turned and walked slowly back to the deck, taking up the place he was to occupy so often during the next four years. Just looking across the water, thinking of Emma.

EMMA'S JOURNEY

Higher and higher the white swallow flew, until Emma felt soft clouds envelop her. It was a comforting feeling, and although for the moment she could not see the little white swallow, she knew she was travelling in the right direction. Then she broke through the cloud into bright sunshine, and in the distance she saw it reflected off a small figure moving above the clouds like a free-wheeling star. Emma knew that she was being held by some unseen thread to the path of the white swallow.

All manner of things passed: an eagle broke through the cloud and dived down through it again, and a flight of martins heading north crossed her path. She gazed ahead to relocate the swallow. There it was still, small, swift and very purposeful. It knew where it was going.

The clouds began to break apart, and Emma glanced below. She could see green paddocks and tiny houses set beside roadways, and occasionally rivers and streams sparkled in the sunshine. A little later, the farms and paddocks were left behind, and she saw that forests covered the land. The cloud shadows drifted slowly, making dark patches over the wooded slopes of the hills. Before long, the hills became higher, the slopes steeper. Then the country levelled again and the trees appeared more scattered, and more spreading in shape, and soft grassy meadows lay between the clusters of trees.

Pools of clear water sparkled, each set amongst emerald grass dotted with tiny yellow and white flowers. As she flew, Emma breathed deeply, filling her spirit with the cool fresh air which carried the scent of the mountains. She felt no fear, just a strong sense of peace and certainty. She knew the white swallow was guiding her path, and she followed unwaveringly.

As she travelled beyond the small plateau with its bright shining pools, great forested valleys opened out beneath her and misty blue ranges rose all around. Two or three high peaks still carried drifts of winter snow, and the air was thin and crystal clear. On and on they flew, the tiny white swallow always visible, the magic thread between them drawing Emma steadily to her spirit home.

The mountains grew higher, their tops lightly wreathed with wisps of cloud, and the long ridges which ran down into the valleys below were deeply etched in purple shadows.

What was that beyond, where the white swallow was heading? Emma's spirit lifted; she knew it was the highest peak of the high wild country jutting through the cloud. Suddenly the white swallow swooped into the cloud, momentarily lost from view. Emma followed and felt again the comfort of the cool whiteness as it enveloped her.

She felt herself descending, and through the mist she glimpsed grey-green treetops, and bright grassy meadows. Huge clusters of rocks were visible here and there, and water sparkled in the late afternoon light. Then she slipped through the cloud, and she knew just where she was.

The little white swallow now flew slowly around her. 'Well, you're home now, Emma. You can choose wherever you want to roam.' It watched Emma's face, with her joyful smile and bright eyes, as she gazed over the wild heathland all about her. The little swallow was satisfied that its mission was complete.

'I'm going to leave you now,' it said. 'I don't know if we'll meet again, but I am sure I will have other spirits to guide to their new homes. Goodbye, Emma, and have a beautiful and peaceful eternity.'

'Goodbye, white swallow, and thank you . . . you knew just where I wanted to come.'

With this, Emma turned her attention to the wide wild country below, deciding just where she would come to rest and start her new life.

The white swallow flew towards the sunset, and Emma caught one quick flash of light as the sun reflected off its wings, and then it was gone.

For the moment Emma was alone.

AARON'S FAREWELL

In essence, Aaron stopped living when Emma died.

For weeks he lay on his bed with a sad, distant look in his eyes. He showed no interest in games, nor did he even want to go for a walk in the forest in the evening after work. Only sometimes would he be a larrikin, when he would pinch Sue's slipper, or the toy possum which sat on the stairs, and deposit them outside on the wet morning grass. It was his way of ensuring that breakfast was on time.

When little Alice came into their lives some time later, it gave him some momentary happiness. She adored him as an older, wise brother, and though she was shy and a little uncertain, he found her gentleness and prettiness somehow comforting. She was company, she was active and busy, and she encouraged him to play now and again, or sat quietly with him if that was what he wanted. In time,

... Sue's slipper and the toy possum ... outside on the wet morning grass ...

he grew to love her dearly, and would welcome her back fondly if they had been separated for any length of time.

Bush trips were still a pleasure. But not like before. And when they went to the high wild country, he would stand, looking and listening, feeling the wind in his face carrying the fragrance of the flowers, and thinking of his mate.

'I know you're here, Em. When my time is up, I'll come to you.'

He knew his time was near, four years later. Although he was still very fit, and went for long walks with Sue and Bill and Alice, he felt a change within himself.

'I think of the high wild country a lot now, Alice. Just like Emma did when her time was up.'

Alice didn't speak. A deep sadness entered her soul. This dear companion, who had quietly taught her so much, and given her security and strength even in the midst of his own pain and loss, was leaving her. She knew he needed to find Emma again, that his spirit was yearning for that love, and her kind and sensitive little heart could only grieve for the loss she knew she and Sue and Bill would feel with his passing.

The morning came. Just as they had with Emma, Sue and Bill carried Aaron gently out onto the deck so he could look across the billabong. As he gazed over the water, he listened to all the familiar sounds which had filled his life. He knew, even as he was leaving it, that the patterns of life would continue, each season bringing its promise of renewal, of the flow of birth and death. He quietly lay watching as the mountain ducks shepherded their new babies out onto the still water of the billabong, as though they knew the time had come to say farewell to the gentle keeper of this place.

'Goodbye, Sue, and Bill. Thank you for all the love and care you have given me. And for Emma, and Alice.' He turned his head to look into both their faces.

Tears rolled down their cheeks. Their faces grew dimmer, their voices faint as he heard them murmur, 'Rest peacefully, darling boy . . . run now with Emma, across the high wild plains.'

His body lay still. And as his spirit began its journey, Aaron felt a quickening. He was going to Emma. He needed no white swallow to guide him. He knew by instinct where she would be. He soared up and up, through the cloud and out into the sunshine. The knowledge that he

... the mountain ducks shepherded their new babies out onto the still water of the billabong ...

would soon be reunited with his mate gave him his direction, and he travelled swiftly through the brightness of the day. As the shadows were lengthening, he found himself looking down on the dear familiar places, the winding streams, the old snow gums, the windswept heath lands and the rocky outcrops which jutted above the shrubs. Not many flowers yet, for there were still patches of late snow lying across the grassy meadows.

I think I know where she might be, he thought, as he alighted on the ground. But he couldn't feel it beneath his paws. It was a strange sensation, and he stood for a while, gathering himself and breathing deeply as the fragrance of the high wild country swept over him.

He guessed that Emma might still be tucked up in one of the caves they used to explore. And then he caught her scent on a breeze rolling down a long gully. Looking up, he saw a group of snow gums growing around a large rock outcrop, and he knew she was there. With mounting excitement, he sped up to the trees. In the rocky outcrop he found the opening he was looking for, a small passage leading to a cave. He had to lower his head to look inside, and as his eyes adjusted to

... he saw her curled up in a tight ball, paws pulled into her chest ...

the dark, he saw her curled up in a tight ball, paws pulled into her chest and the familiar, loved head tucked into them.

He watched her for a few moments and then, moving forward slowly, he touched his nose lightly to the fur on the top of her head. Her scent flooded back to him. She stirred and slowly turned so that their noses touched. Instantly she was awake.

REUNION

‘Aaron, Aaron! It’s really you! It’s not just a dream!’

All in one movement, she unwound herself, jumped up and woofed excitedly. Aaron backed out of the cave to allow her to come out.

‘Aaron!’ she cried joyously, as she ran round and round in a dance of happiness, ‘I knew you were coming, I just knew it!’

‘Emma, Emma, slow down for a minute . . . I’m getting dizzy watching you!’

They both laughed, as she dropped onto the ground, rolling in the patch of snow nearby, still quivering with joy.

Aaron joined with her in the happiness of their reunion, barking, running, dodging, picking up sticks and throwing them into the air. Gradually, their joy in finding each other again became calmer, as they realised that they were together again, forever this time.

Sitting close, they began to tell each

Aaron joined with her in the happiness of their reunion, barking, running, dodging ...

other about the things that had happened since their separation.

'I was lonely for a long time,' Emma said, 'even though I was so happy being here, I missed you and Sue and Bill so much. Not having you with me meant I had to have all the new experiences on my own. I wondered what I would find to eat, and then I realised that I was never hungry. It saves a lot of time not having to hunt. And I only need to drink water in summer, when the snows have gone — just to refresh my spirit. Sometimes I eat soft snow if I wake up during the winter.'

'Isn't it cold then?' asked Aaron. 'Where do you sleep?'

'Well,' she replied, 'you don't feel hot or cold. But it's often snowing hard, so I've spent the last four winters in a cave deep in the rocks. It's really cosy. I often have the company of tiny possums, and they go into a deep sleep for all the time the snow covers the country.

'In summer, I often go with them into the night while they hunt moths and beetles, and apart from the wombats and the hares and dingoes, and an occasional fox, they are my main company. But I'm never lonely now. I watch the flowers coming out as the snow retreats, and I know all the birds, and when the cattle come up to the high country I pretend I'm back home "oofing" them, like you and I used to do.

'But tell me what you've been doing since I left, and about Sue and Bill, and the bush trips you've been on. There was one time — oh, a while back, perhaps two snows ago — when I was way over on the big hill looking back up the valley, and I thought I saw the Landrover driving along the road, but it didn't stop. It was late and I couldn't follow you. There was one other time when I thought I saw you all, and there was another Airedale there too.'

In truth, though she did not want to tell him, there had been several occasions when she had seen Sue and Bill and Aaron. The first time, she had run joyously up to greet them, only to find that they could not see her and did not know she was there. Her disappointment was so great, she was heartbroken. Only later did she realise that she was now invisible to them. Her sad recollections were interrupted by Aaron's answer.

'Yes,' he said, 'we did come up here a few times, and Sue and Bill talked about you often, wondering if you were happy and if you could sense our presence. The other one is little Alice. When you had to leave us, I was so sad and lonely, and very unhappy for Sue and Bill, because they cried a lot at losing you. They have never stopped talking and thinking about you, and how much they miss you. But somehow they found Alice for me so that I would have company. She has been very good for them too.

'She came from where I did. In fact, I heard Sue and Bill saying that she is my grand-niece. I think that's something to do with my sister's daughter, or her daughter, so I suppose she's part of my clan.'

Emma looked at him. 'What about your pain? Did Alice help that?'

He thought for a long while, sniffing at a new scent drifting on the breeze.

'Partly . . . yes. She was company and full of fun, and she loved me, that was plain to see.

'But . . . but I saw you in everything she did. Perhaps I was too old for her then, past "bashups" and games like that. But she is very sweet, and she did make my life better. She was company if Sue and Bill were away. And besides, I had to pass the knowledge on before it was time for me to leave. She learnt quickly and now she knows just as much as we did.'

'Will she be as lonely as we were without each other?'

Aaron thought for a moment as his gaze followed a flock of rosellas flying overhead, seeking their evening roosting tree.

'No, I don't think so. She'll be sad, but she'll have a stronger bond with Sue and Bill now that she's on her own.'

Emma seemed satisfied with this, for even though she didn't know Alice, she was a part of the great Airedale clan, each a part of the greater whole, and what affected one affected them all.

She had much to show Aaron in his new home, and he had much to learn. It would be her responsibility and joy to lead him into these new experiences, but not today. She was at peace now, just being close beside him in their high wild country of flowers and meadows and rocks and water.

She had waited such a long time for him to come to her, and she would savour it now.

Tomorrow would be the start of their new life together.

TIME TOGETHER

It was now early summer, and as the months passed, they renewed their bonds of love and companionship. Together they explored the high wild country that was their home. There were moments of joy as they visited favourite places, places which held special memories of Sue and Bill, times when the four of them had walked all day glorying in the freedom of these wild moorlands. They remembered the long evenings around the warmth of the camp fire in their own particular snow plain where Sue and Bill always liked to camp, and how Emma especially liked to be lifted up for a cuddle before bedtime. And in the morning, there was always plenty of buttered toast for breakfast, before setting off for another day of exploring amongst the high rocky knolls and the hidden glens and valleys, and the pools and streams that lay shining in the sun.

They talked about all the things Aaron had done since Emma's passing, all the places he had been, the training and

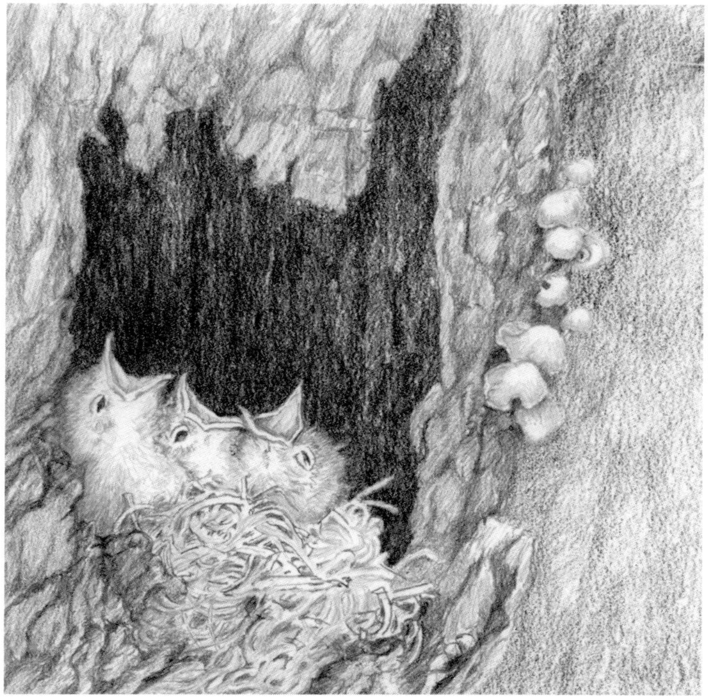

She told him how many nests she had found ...

teaching of Alice, and Sue and Bill's happiness and sadness. And Emma showed him all her resting places, where she had once slept all winter with a gentle black snake, and told him how many wrens' and robins' nests she had found. She took him to the rock outcrop above the pretty lake in their favourite valley, where they sat most evenings watching the birds feeding, and the fish rising, until darkness came.

They explored faraway places that were new even to Emma, but avoided by instinct any contact with people walking across the plains. They were at peace with each other again, as they had been before, and thoughts of Sue and Bill were now further back in their minds, though they were not forgotten.

They didn't actually need to sleep very often, and even when curled up for winter, they were just at peace with their surroundings. Spirit forces played over them, giving them knowledge and wisdom from the world about them, preparing them for a greater involvement in it. There was no need for finding food (though Aaron said his stomach still rumbled sometimes), and the clear stream water or snow was always at hand.

They measured time by the passage of the seasons. The warm bright days and clear star-studded nights of summer, with occasional crashing mountain storms, gradually gave way to autumn. Often, as a late summer day became still and cool, and the sky cleared of cloud, they would sit and watch the yellow and pink of the western sky, as the sun sank to its resting place. They would hear a little family of ringtail possums emerging into the soft evening light, scampering along the branches of the snow gums like tiny trapeze artists to drink from the nectar-

The delicate white gentians of the marshes bloomed shyly ...

filled blossoms crowding the grey-foliaged branches. Long after their silhouetted bodies had blended into the night, their busy foraging noises and twittering calls could be heard. So too the distant calls of a mopoke owl seeking his mate echoed from the dense timber below the snowline.

The delicate white gentians of the marshes bloomed shyly, always the last of the summer flowers, and Emma and Aaron knew that the first silent snow-flakes would fall any day soon. Early one quiet morning, they awoke to find the grassy meadows spread with a white quilt, and the branches of the old snow gums bowed beneath their first snowy capes. For most of that first winter together, they chose to curl up in a favourite cave, knowing that they were cocooned in snow, but not feeling cold.

Sometimes, they lay quietly with eyes closed, thinking their own thoughts, mostly about Sue and Bill and home, and of the happy times when they were all together. At other times, they would talk about these things, reliving past journeys for days and days.

Emma would often begin with, 'Aaron, 'member when we . . . ?'

And Aaron would smile, and say, 'Yes, Em . . . it was fun, wasn't it?'

He loved the way she was so fond of 'membering' things.

Occasionally, on nights of full moon, they would leave the cave and walk across the snow, silver in the moonshine spreading over it. Very little stirred; all the birds had migrated to the lowlands, as had the dingoes. Once they saw a fox making hard work of walking across the snow, which was halfway up his legs. Aaron looked behind where he and Emma had walked, and they had not even left a paw print.

It was a strange sensation to feel a total part of this environment, their home, but at the same time to feel above it. He could see Emma and feel the touch of her nose on his, or her body against him when they slept, but no other animal paid them any heed. He was to find out why some months later, when the snow had once again retreated from the mountains, and the streams rushed with clear new water.

SCATTERING THE ASHES

As he lifted his head from drinking deeply in the cold clear stream, Aaron surveyed the surrounding country now bathed in the light of a new day.

'You know, Emma, I do enjoy moving through the late night and watching and listening to the sounds of sunrise.' He drew a deep breath, the chill air fragrant and sharp.

She too paused a moment from drinking, the water dripping like diamonds from her whiskers. 'I always feel part of the change, Aaron, like a guardian, you might say. I'm happy when the night creatures are tucked up for the day, and the ones who have slept during the night start to get busy.'

He loved hearing Emma speak in this 'mothering' way, as if the care of all creatures was her responsibility. It was part of why he loved her so deeply.

He bent his head again for another drink, but stopped suddenly and glanced over his shoulder. 'Did you hear that, Em? It sounded like a human voice.'

They had seen and heard a few hardy walkers in this rugged country, but this voice was different. It was familiar.

'I didn't, Aaron, but my mind was probably elsewhere.'

'I was dreaming, I suppose,' he said, as he resumed drinking.

But there it was again, a man's voice, and this time Emma heard it too.

'You're right, Aaron, and it's not far away . . . I think it's behind that low wooded hill.'

'My heart — why is it beating so fast?' Aaron asked himself.

Just then two figures came into view around the slope of the hill. He knew them immediately.

'Emma! Look! It's Sue and Bill, they've come to find us! We'll all be together again!' He barked in greeting. 'Come on, Em, let's go and meet them! I didn't think we'd see them so soon.'

He started to run in great strides towards the approaching figures. Emma hesitated, and as she did she saw a third figure running in circles across the landscape.

'That must be Alice. She runs just like I used to when I first came here.'

But she didn't rush after Aaron. There was something she knew from her own sad experience, and that he was about to find out for himself.

Alice, who was now between Aaron and Sue and Bill, suddenly stopped her running and stood with one front paw poised. She had sensed something nearby. That's strange, she thought. I can feel something — someone close, but I can't see anything. She was uncertain, but a longing stirred within her.

'Look at Alice, she's caught a scent,' said Bill. 'Probably a hare — she loves to flush them out.'

Aaron, who was close to Alice, barked a further greeting, wagging his tail hard. He stopped suddenly, puzzled.

She's not hearing me, he thought. 'Alice!' he barked, 'It's me, Aaron!'

He stood confused, and turned to Emma, who had joined him. 'Why doesn't she know me? I feel as if she's looking right through me.'

He ran on the few paces to the steadily walking couple. 'Sue, Bill, why doesn't Alice know me? It's us, Aaron and Emma . . . aren't you pleased to see us?'

But neither seemed to see or hear him, and they just kept walking. Alice resumed her activities though she stopped often, looking around to sniff the air. Aaron stood still and dejected as they walked away in the direction from which he and Emma had just come.

'Have they forgotten us so soon, Emma? They didn't seem to know we were here.'

Emma stood with him as they sadly watched the figures recede in the distance.

'They didn't know, Aaron. They can't see us now we're spirits, even though we can see them and hear what they say.'

'But Alice stopped and looked, she knew we were here,' he cried, a feeling of great sadness overwhelming him.

'Yes, I know,' said Emma. 'But it was her deeper instincts which sensed us near. She just couldn't work out what it was.'

Emma sympathised with the sadness her soul mate was feeling. 'This happened to me too, Aaron, when you all came up here after I had passed into the spirit world. I was as confused as you were, and I had no-one to explain it to me, no companion to ease my pain.'

'But Sue and Bill always said we'd be with you again one day in the high country,' he said sadly as he watched the disappearing pair. 'How can this be so if they didn't even see us?'

She knew he was feeling a deep hurt. She leaned against him and licked his ear a few times.

'Aaron, what they meant was they would be with us when they too pass out of the earthly life into the spirit world we live in.' She paused while he considered this. 'It may be some time, in fact a long time. But one day, in the mists of the future, we will all be together.' She paused again, as she felt his body relax. 'And then no-one will separate us again, ever.'

There was a long silence. Then he gave a deep sigh.

'Thank you, Emma. I feel happier now that I realise it will happen one day. And of course we'll see them lots of times when they come up here walking.'

They were on their own again now, but Aaron was not yet ready to lose the contact.

'Let's follow them and see where they go, and what they do. That way at least we can still share time with them.'

Together they rose and loped in the direction the trio had taken. They soon caught up and fell into step beside them.

'They seem to be heading somewhere in particular. It's almost as if this visit has a special purpose,' Emma said. Aaron didn't reply. He was still feeling a bit shaken. They were approaching a bend in the valley where the creek opened to a broad slow-moving stretch. Bill and Sue stopped and, calling Alice to them, they set down a small box which Sue had taken from her backpack.

'Sit quietly, Alice,' said Bill. And from habit, Aaron and Emma sat too. 'We've got something special to do,' Bill went on. Aaron and Emma watched, as Sue and Bill opened the box. They each scooped up a small quantity of something Aaron and Emma could not see.

'Wouldn't it be good, Bill, if it went all the way down the valley?' said Sue quietly. 'This was one of their most favourite places, along this creek.' Silently they allowed whatever it was in their hands to trickle onto the surface of the water.

Emma felt a deep sadness as she looked at the silent pair kneeling on the cushiony grass, Bill with his arm around Sue's shoulders. She saw they were both crying. Alice rose and moved to sniff the contents of the box. Then she moved away and lay by herself, looking along the creek as it wound its way down the valley.

Sue spoke. 'We know their spirits are here, Bill. Now we have returned part of their bodies to their spirit home.'

Together they all sat, watching as the shadows lengthened behind them to the east. The day was closing in. Words passed between Sue and Bill which Emma and Aaron couldn't quite hear, and then they stood up. With one last look down the valley, they called Alice to them and set off back to where they had come from.

Aaron was tempted to follow, but Emma's voice cut across his thoughts. 'I wonder what they put in the water? It looked like powder falling through their fingers.'

Rising, they walked to the stream edge and scanned the surface of the pool.

'I can't see much, Em, just some small particles caught in an eddy under that bank down there.'

'Whatever it was, Aaron, it meant a lot to them and they were very sad.'

They were not to know that when Aaron had died, Bill and Sue had

It looked like powder falling through their fingers ...

recovered Emma's body from its grave and arranged for the two to be cremated. Their ashes were in the small box which Sue had carried.

Aaron felt a sadness himself, but so that Emma wouldn't dwell upon it, he said, 'Come on then, we've still got to get down to the lake edge before dark.'

'Yes, of course we do,' said Emma, her thoughts now on more immediate issues. 'The wood duck babies may have hatched and we wanted to see them find a new home on the lake. Let's have a last drink and hurry off.' As they dipped their heads to the water and lapped at its cool sweetness, some of the powdery particles came with it, and were absorbed into their spirits.

As Emma moved downstream, Aaron turned for a final view of the three figures, now all but blended into the shadows of distant snow gums.

I still feel sad, he thought, but a different sadness from before. And I also know that one day nothing will separate us.

As he turned to follow his beloved Emma, his mind conjured up images of the five of them roaming for ever across these vast and beautiful wild high plains.

THE RIPPLING FLOWERS

At the first melting of the snow, something strange happened beneath the shallow icy waters. A flower started to bloom.

Every year, Aaron and Emma came to an ice cavern to watch this beautiful event. The drinking of the first snow melt was also a ritual for them, a renewal of the spirit after the long snow-bound winter.

Because the flowers opened under water, there was constant movement of the petals which, although they did not understand it, fascinated them. The flutter of the flowers increased as they drank.

Emma called them her 'rippling flowers', and because they signalled the start of the long wild-flower season which they both loved so much, they were her favourite.

Oh, but when the patches of sky lilies opened their delicate ice-blue faces among the damp grass, they too became her favourite. And when the sweet fruity fragrance from the carpets of creamy-yellow stackhousia flowers wafted to her later in the season on warm days, her earlier favourites were temporarily supplanted.

Yellow had always been Aaron's favourite colour. He remembered how, when he was a baby puppy, all those years ago, he would help Sue in the nursery with her plants, and he always showed her where the yellow flowers were. He would pick the flowers off the plants and waddle his baby way across to present them to her.

Up here on the high plains, there was no shortage of flowers in his special colour. All through late spring, summer and autumn, a multitude of daisies followed one another in shades of palest creamy-yellow or deep gold to the vivid orange bobble heads of the billy buttons which grew thickly in the grassy meadows and beside the streams. Sometimes Aaron and Emma would lie on beds of fluffy yellow kunzea, which carpeted large rocks like big doonas. Although he could not nip off their flowers like he did as a puppy, he still revelled in the warm fragrance and soft foliage.

The snow gums were amongst Aaron's favourites too. He never tired of the sight of those satin-sheened twisty-limbed trees which looked old even when they were young, and which gave cool dappled shade to the daisies and buttercups clustered about their gnarled bases in the thick soft grass. He and Emma loved to lie in the grass, eyes closed but noses a-twitch as the warm perfumes caressed them on the breezes.

While Emma simply enjoyed things for what they were, Aaron liked to record his observations in his mind. He well remembered Bill saying something about how plants had to set their buds and flowers quickly between the snows, because there wasn't much time from last snow-melt to first snowfall. Some plants even took a different way. They would set their buds but then stay dormant, or 'asleep' as Bill said, right through winter, ready to burst into full flower once the warmth and light of early spring and summer surrounded them again.

Aaron didn't know how those little buds managed to survive the blizzards and icy winds for all those months, but there was no doubt that Bill was right. He saw it happen himself. This knowledge made his wanderings before and after the snows fell even more interesting.

And so they passed their summers, roaming over wooded hills and through

Emma called them her 'rippling flowers' ...

broad valleys, across which little creeks and streams curled and wound their ways to the edges of the great high plains, where they tumbled and fell in cascades to join the big rivers flowing eventually to the oceans. And all the time they marked the season's progress by what was in flower.

LET'S GO SKIING

Sometimes, Aaron and Emma would have the urge to travel. After all, there was no limit to where they could go, and they could stay away as long as they liked.

'I don't often look for company, Aaron, but can we go to those mountains in the east and watch the people skiing?' Emma asked early one morning, well before the sun was up.

He thought for a moment. 'Why not? I was just thinking yesterday that we tend to stay in our caves a lot when the snow is everywhere . . . yes, let's.'

Together they rose, and in a moment were high above the snowy plains, heading east to where the sun was just climbing into the sky. The whiteness below flushed rosy pink, then gold, and the shadows of the old snow-laden gums spread out their arms across the dips and hollows. A couple of currawongs flew beneath them, eyes keenly watching for morsels of food below. A little flame robin flashed into the sheltering foliage of the friendly gums, his breast a tiny brilliant beacon to his mate.

The sun grew warmer, and the light brighter as they descended to the sparkly expanse of snow where already dozens of early skiers, dressed in vivid snow suits, were gathering on the slopes that rose above the village.

'They do look very small from up here,' said Emma. 'Let's go down and see them up close.'

Aaron and Emma glided just above the busy scene. Already it was noisy with the lifts and tows carrying skiers to the very top of the mountain ridge, from where they could then choose a way down various slopes. Some people were using two skis, others a bigger single ski, and on lower slopes in a special area, children were tumbling about on toboggans or sheets of plastic, squealing and giggling as they rolled in the snow.

'It looks like fun going down the steep slopes, Aaron. How about we have a go?'

Aaron saw the gleam in Emma's eyes. He knew how much she was enjoying this change of activity. They alighted where many people were standing in queues, awaiting their turn to go down the slopes.

'Come on Aaron, no-one will see us, let's jump the line.'

Not wanting to spoil her fun, he moved through the crowd and stopped at the top of a long steep run.

'It looks very steep, Aaron.'

'You're not having second thoughts, Em, are you?' said Aaron, his eyes twinkling.

'Certainly not! I'll beat you to the bottom!'

And with this, she leapt onto the slope, sat on her haunches and off she went. Aaron followed. As they picked up speed, they passed some of the skiers. The wind rushed past their ears, brisk and fresh.

'This is really fun!' Emma was gaining confidence. 'But we do seem to be going very fast!'

So fast, in fact, that because there was no friction holding them back, they outstripped all the skiers.

Near the bottom, Emma rolled herself into a ball and tumbled over and over until she came to rest in a pile of snow. When Aaron caught up with her, she was lying in the snow laughing and laughing at the pleasure of the slide.

'Oh,' she said, 'that was such fun. Let's do it again.'

And they did, time and time again, until daylight faded, and the skiers one by one left the slopes, going back to the warm cosy chalets in the village.

Emma and Aaron sat on the now deserted slopes, happy together as the stars began twinkling in the clear night sky. The moon rose slowly, its great smiling face broad and serene as its soft light cast shadows of rocks and mounds across the snow. But the two companions cast no shadows.

'Well, Emmy . . . happy with your day?' Aaron asked.

'It was wonderful fun, Aaron. Thank you for coming with me,' she said. Looking around at the lights now shining from the chalet windows, she turned to him. 'But now I'm ready to go home.'

He smiled at her and nodded. And so, travelling swiftly, they were soon curled up together in one of the many caves which dotted their own special high wild country. In moments, they were sound asleep.

'It was wonderful fun, Aaron … but now I'm ready to go home ...'

CHARLIE AND ROSE

As they settled down on a knoll at the end of a long walk one day, Aaron noticed the sky to the south growing dark.

'Might be a storm on the way, Em. In fact, I just saw some lightning flash then.'

Emma looked toward the mounting clouds, and nodded. She had never liked storms, ever, and was comforted in the knowledge that a favourite cave was nearby for shelter.

Several kilometres away, a Landrover was parked at the end of a rough track, a little below the tree line of the great high plains. Two Airedales were inside the vehicle. Their names were Charlie and Rose.

Charlie and Rose belonged to a family called Waters. Mr and Mrs Waters, and their two children, Peter and Kate, were away for the afternoon walking in an area where dogs were not permitted. Charlie and Rose didn't mind too much. They had had a good long walk yesterday, and were quite content to rest.

Rose was sitting in the front seat. 'I don't like the look of those black clouds, Charlie . . . I'm sure I heard thunder then,' she said.

Charlie heard it too. He knew how much Rose hated the huge sounds; her ears were so sensitive that the noise could actually hurt.

The next clap of thunder was even closer, almost overhead. Rose shot up in the seat, panting nervously and trembling.

'Steady on, Rosie,' said Charlie in his calmest voice. 'We know it can't hurt us in here.'

But she didn't hear him. As it thundered again, she dived to the floor of the Landrover and crouched beneath the steering wheel, shaking all over so that even the name tag on her collar rattled. Lightning flashes lit up the inside of the vehicle, and thunder surrounded them.

Charlie ducked down, but Rose sprang back onto the seat. Her collar became hooked on the door handle. 'I'm caught, Charlie, I'm caught!' She struggled frantically, pulling this way and that.

'Stay still, Rose, I'll try and get you fr—' but he didn't finish the sentence. The door flew open and Rose tumbled onto the ground. Lightning flashed again, lighting up the tree trunks and momentarily blinding Charlie. Rose bolted up the track.

'Rose, Rose! Wait for me! You don't know where you're going!' he barked. But it was no use. Rose was terrified beyond reason.

She's heading right into the storm. It will only be worse for her, thought Charlie. He realised he must follow fast, or he might lose her forever. He jumped through the still open door and followed her, even though he knew that he should stay by the car until the family returned.

They, however, were several kilometres from the car when the storm broke, and took shelter in a cattlemen's hut until it abated. It was nearly two hours before they returned, to find Charlie and Rose gone.

Not having any idea in which direction the two dogs might have run, they decided to spread out and search for the remaining hour or so of light, and to meet back at the car at nightfall.

When they gathered back together, with no good news, they decided to camp the night and spend the next day searching. They felt sure they would find Charlie and Rose; surely they couldn't have gone too far.

Rose was in a state of terror as she fled. The thunder kept crashing, booming through her highly sensitive ears; she just kept running, without caring where, hoping she could leave the storm behind.

In the occasional lulls in the storm she thought she heard Charlie barking, but there was no time or thought to respond. Fortunately when he did bark, he seemed to be following her. The rain still pelted down, even though the thunder and lightning were fading.

Gradually her fear left her. She was tired and slowed to a loping gait, eventually stopping to drink from a rock pool. There was Charlie's bark again. She turned and barked in response.

They were not to know, but Aaron heard that bark in the distance and knew it was not the dingoes that he and Emma so often heard. 'Did you hear that?' he asked Emma.

'Hear what?' she asked, just as Rose barked again, this time followed by a second bark a little further away. 'There seems to be two of them,' said Aaron, 'and one is close by; let's go and see who it is.'

Silently and without disturbing the

heathland, they loped in the direction of the barking. There it was again, and again, both much closer, and within minutes they saw Rose crouching beside the rock pool, ears lifted, facing away from them.

They stopped. They saw Charlie appear over the rim of the rock and run towards Rose. She wagged her tail even though she was too tired to stand and greet her partner. They touched noses as Airedales always do. 'You're safe,' he said.

'Yes; but I'm very tired and cold,' Rose replied. 'I just want to sleep.'

Aaron and Emma watched this affectionate reunion, and wondered at seeing another pair of Airedales. Where did they come from? Where was their family? Possibly a long way away, thought Aaron, remembering how fierce the storm had been, and how frightening it could be. 'They've probably run for a long time, Emma; it really is a big distance from the road, if that's where they came from. We'd better see what they do and keep an eye on them. They'll probably get hungry soon, but it's nearly dark so they're not going to find much to eat now.' Emma agreed, and the two moved up a little closer to Charlie and Rose.

Charlie was concerned for Rose because he had never seen her as tired as this before. He decided to find a dry shelter where she could be warm for the night, particularly if the storm returned.

He spotted a rocky outcrop beyond where they were resting and, setting off, he led her towards it. It was larger than he thought and there was a broad, dry overhang with shrubs protecting the opening. Dry grass and leaf litter lay on the floor, making a comfortable bed for them. 'We might be very hungry by the morning,' he said to his exhausted mate, wondering what they would find to eat at first light, 'but we'll be dry and warm under here if it rains again.' And it did rain for most of the night, although neither of them noticed it too much as they slept back to back, soon drying out and becoming warm.

'We'd better stay here for the night ourselves, Aaron,' Emma suggested, 'and see if they can find some food in the morning. They'll need it by then.' Not having to worry about getting cold or wet, they curled up not far from the entrance to the overhang to wait for morning. Time did not matter, and while there would be no stars tonight, there were plenty of

Charlie spotted a rocky outcrop beyond where they were resting ...

night noises, including those from two very deeply sleeping Airedales in their rocky haven.

They discussed what the new pair would do when they woke up (which Aaron guessed would be early, seeing they'd had no tea) and wondered whether they would be able to find their way back to where they came from, and how he and Emma could help them find some food. The night passed, as did two wombats, a fox which kept its distance, a more curious dingo, and an owl, which perched on the outcrop until dawn.

NEW TERRITORY

Rose was the first to wake. Coming out into the open, she stretched her stiff body and looked around at the unfamiliar surroundings as she squatted for a pee. When Charlie arose soon after, he was both aware and cautious of the smells of the animals that had passed in the night.

His sense of territory was fully aroused. Deliberately, he went from rock to rock, marking as he went.

Satisfied that he had claimed a new domain, his thoughts turned to food. But what and where?

'I'm really hungry, Charlie,' Rose said.

That's strange, thought Charlie to himself, because she isn't that keen on breakfast and I usually have to finish it up.

Looking around at the expanse of country with its mantle of windswept dwarfed shrubs, he wondered where to start looking. Searching around the outcrop, he could find only dead beetles and grasshoppers and moths, at which he turned up his nose. Moving out into the dense vegetation he searched for a long time, but with even less success. Returning to Rose, he had to admit failure, and began to think that the hard insect carcasses might be better than nothing.

He led Rose to where some storm-battered grasshoppers and beetles lay dead on the rocks. She showed no interest in these unappetising offerings, but hunger drove her to experiment. She picked up a beetle, and chewed and rolled it around her mouth, thinking how tasteless it was. Eventually she managed to swallow it. She looked at a large furry moth and decided to try this instead of any more beetles. It was only freshly dead, and as she bit into it a slightly sweet oil was released from the body.

'Try one of these,' she said to Charlie, who had been chewing steadily, but without relish, on his third beetle. The first bite of the moth made him realise that these were better value, and as there were numerous piles of dead moths around the rocks, he and Rose had soon eaten enough to satisfy their hunger.

They had not noticed as they ate that a fresh storm was building up. A few drops of rain fell, and Charlie saw that while the dark sky approached them from one direction, in the other it was still clear and light.

'I think we'd better head that way, Rose. I'm not sure where we are but I don't think that it's a good idea to be here when that storm comes.'

'All right,' she agreed. 'Let's go now. I feel rested and I'm not hungry anymore.'

Aaron and Emma, who had listened and watched with some amusement as the pair experimented with their new diet, were a bit dismayed by their decision to move, because it was away from the direction from which they had come.

'If they leave, I think we had better follow them to make sure they're all right,' said Aaron. Emma nodded.

And so the four Airedales loped down from the rise, heading towards a snow-gum woodland some kilometres away. Once or twice Charlie looked back to see how far the storm was behind them, but it wasn't moving fast and they kept well ahead of it. It was not only to look back at the storm though. He had the strongest feeling that they were not alone in that vast wilderness, but when he turned his head there was nobody behind them.

After about an hour, Rose said, 'Can we stop for a while? I'm a bit tired, and the storm doesn't seem any closer.' She was in fact hungry again, and thirsty, and she could smell water not too far ahead. When they reached it, they found that it was a winding stream. Shallow pools lay in depressions in the curve of the stream meanders, and they waded into one of these to drink, and to cool off a little.

'What's this?' Charlie said. 'Look, Rose, there's lots of small fish in this pool. They seem to have just died.'

It was true. As the pool receded, small trout had been trapped, and now were dying from lack of oxygen in the water.

They watched as a raven alighted by the edge of the pool and, tentatively wading into a shallow part, reached out and plucked a small dead fish, then flew off.

'Wow, Rose, real breakfast,' he said.

'Yes,' she responded as they gleefully stepped into the shallow section of the pool. There were dozens of fish, either dead or nearly so, and the two Airedales had no trouble catching enough to satisfy their hunger.

Their invisible guardians followed and watched as Charlie and Rose, now moving more slowly as the threat of the storm diminished, investigated their new

Their invisible guardians followed and watched Charlie and Rose ...

surroundings, sniffing here and there. Once a hare darted from a bush at their feet, and they spent the next few minutes running in circles, criss-crossing its scent, while the hare silently headed away in a safe direction.

REMEMBERING

As he watched Charlie and Rose, Aaron's thoughts turned to the early visits he and Emma had made to these great high plains with Sue and Bill, when he knew so strongly that this was their spirit home. Was Emma thinking the same, he wondered, as he turned and saw her eyes following the pair as they ran easily across the heath-lands. Would Charlie and Rose also find their spiritual link with this storm-swept, wild landscape?

'Emma,' he said.

'Yes, Aaron?' she responded with a start as if she had been woken suddenly.

'I was wondering. . .' he began, 'I wondered if you were seeing us again — in Charlie and Rose, I mean. Look at them running from smell to smell, wading into the pools and creeks, drinking as though they'd never stop, sniffing around every rocky outcrop . . .'

'Yes, I was, actually,' she said with a little smile in her eyes. 'And I was thinking how clever those hares are at avoiding hunters like us . . . like we used to be, I mean.'

They sat silently for a few moments.

'We never did catch one, did we, Em?'

'No. . . I was thinking too, about when the four of us, you, me and Sue and Bill, would all lie in the sun on the soft grass, and watch the eagles circling above, catching the wind we couldn't see.'

'Yes, and when Sue and Bill found a new plant they hadn't seen, or a patch of snow daisies like a garden under the old snow gums . . . how happy they looked.'

Lost in thoughts, they had not really noticed the mist creeping silently up through the trees, long fingers drifting out onto the heathlands. They even had trouble seeing Charlie and Rose, who were only about fifty metres ahead of them.

'We'd better catch up, Aaron, and stay nearby. Even if we can't show them which way they should go, we'll at least know where they're heading,' said Emma.

In no time they were just behind Charlie and Rose, and instead of staying

'This looks a good place, Rose, and there might be some more fish for the morning ...'

back, joined them to watch more closely what they were sniffing out.

'That's funny,' said Charlie, stopping his searching, and looking from side to side. 'Can you feel that there's something here with us? I don't know what it is, but I can feel something strange.'

Rose could see the erect hair on the back of his neck, and while she did not feel it as strongly, she did sense 'something' was nearby. 'I can't see anything, but I think I know what you mean,' she replied. Slightly puzzled, they continued their wanderings across the heathland.

By late afternoon, the mist was changing into a colder night fog, and although they did not realise it, they had run and wandered about twenty kilometres since morning. For the past hour they had been dropping down a long steep slope. Tall straight trees had replaced the squat contorted snow gums and the vegetation, which earlier had brushed their lower legs, now sometimes blocked their view.

Fortunately, they weren't hungry. Just before they had started their descent into the valley, they had found another pool with fish in it, and had also found a large cluster of plump moths around a rocky outcrop.

Rose was tired, and Charlie kept a lookout for a likely night spot before it became too dark. Large rocky outcrops weren't as common as up on the plains, but as it was much warmer down here and didn't look like rain, a cave was not so essential for their camp tonight.

They heard the sound of water rushing over rocks, and as they were thirsty again they made for the noise. Soon they broke out of the bush onto a stream bank. Large flat boulders jutted out over the rushing water, which tumbled and cascaded into a large pool. A broad smooth ledge near the water's edge was partly sheltered by dense bushes.

'This looks a good place, Rose, and there might be some more fish for the morning.'

Too tired to even respond, Rose flopped onto the ledge, had a large drink of the cold clean water, and settled down to rest. After he too had drunk, Charlie sat beside her and watched the night close in. A pair of wallabies came to drink on the opposite bank, and even though they sniffed the air, the new scent didn't seem to worry them greatly. Rose was well asleep when Charlie eventually lay down beside her some hours later.

A pair of wallabies came to drink on the opposite bank ...

The sky had cleared suddenly and, even though it was colder, he watched the stars grow brighter, and saw the water of the stream sparkle silver as the moon rose into the clear night. He felt relaxed, with a sense of belonging, comfortable with his surroundings, although he was concerned for Rose, for he had never known her to tire so easily. He would have to make sure she had enough food and stayed here until she was strong again.

Aaron and Emma watched the night moods along with Charlie and noted the change in his body; he was more relaxed, and seemed a part of his surroundings. They looked at one another knowingly.

THE PLAY GROUNDS

Over the next two days Charlie and Rose moved only a little way from the creek until Rose seemed stronger. They found enough 'hard food' and even berries on some bushes which, though small, were sweet and plentiful.

'Rose, do you feel strong enough to climb back up to the plains? We really need to go up high again to find our way back to the family,' said Charlie.

'Yes, I'm much better now, Charlie.' Rose looked up from a patch of berries she was nibbling. 'I think you're right, we should try.'

They climbed slowly, stopping often, and slept two more nights on the way before the tall trees were well behind them and the vegetation was becoming stunted again.

'Rose,' began Charlie, then he stopped.

'What is it, Charlie?'

'I'm just wondering . . . what if we can't find our family again? What will we do?'

Rose was silent.

'Well,' she said eventually, 'we've got water, we know we can find food, and there's plenty of shelter for when the weather's bad. Why don't we find ourselves a safe place to live for a while?'

Charlie smiled at Rose, and touched her on the nose. He was relieved that she was not worrying too much. He had thought she might panic if they were really unable to find their way back. He felt very responsible for them both.

They had almost reached the head of the creek, where it cascaded between steep banks. Beyond, slightly higher up, the country opened out into a wide basin. They paused on the edge of the stream and looked towards a large rocky outcrop, tucked amongst gnarled snow gums. The stream they had been following seemed to spring from near the base of one very large rock.

'What a beautiful place, Charlie!' exclaimed Rose. Her gaze wandered over the broad valley, carpeted with soft grass and sprinkled with buttercups and daisies. 'If there's a big cave in those rocks, why don't we stay? I feel happy here.'

Charlie thought for a few moments. He felt a little uncertain. Part of him knew they should keep looking for the family, but he too felt very happy in this place.

'OK, Rose,' he said. 'Let's go and look. If there is a cave, perhaps we could stay for a while.'

And there was. The rocky outcrop rose above the shrubs, large boulders clustered about its base. Investigating closely, Charlie and Rose found a gap among the boulders and, following a sort of tunnel, they discovered a deep weatherproof cavern. The floor was dry, covered lightly with leaves and dry grass, and the walls showed no signs of dampness. It smelled fresh and cool, so there was plenty of air.

'This is really snug, Charlie. I wonder if it has been used by other animals before?'

'Maybe, Rose . . . but I don't think anyone's been here for quite a while. It smells nice and clean. Are you really sure you want to stay, though?'

'Well . . . yes, Charlie. I am. I think we are so far away now that we may never be able to find our way back, and perhaps it would be best if we made a little home straight away.'

There was something else on her mind, though she didn't tell Charlie. She would soon, but not yet.

She had realised yesterday that her tiredness was due to something quite unexpected: she was pregnant. She had noticed when rolling on her back in the bristly heath that her teats had suddenly swollen. Charlie had not noticed yet, but Rose knew that before long he would have to spend a lot of time searching for food, and that they would need a safe and sheltered place to live. This lovely little valley was just right.

Aaron and Emma had followed Charlie and Rose all the way. They knew this valley well themselves; it was a favourite sitting and thinking place, and they loved it. They called it the Play Grounds. It was well away from any bushwalking tracks and the animals who came to drink at the spring, morning and night, were gentle and unafraid.

'Aaron, I think Charlie and Rose are going to stay here, by the look of it,' said Emma. 'It's a safe home for them, and they are going to need it, too.'

There was something in her tone that made Aaron take more notice.

'Why do you say it like that, Em?'

'Well, Rose is going to have puppies. Not straight away, but soon, I'm pretty sure.'

Aaron looked at her admiringly. 'How do you know these things, Emma? I bet even Charlie doesn't know.'

Emma smiled at him. 'Oh,' she said, 'it's just one of those things . . . girls know.'

The afternoon shadows were growing longer. Charlie and Rose spent some time looking around their new home, happy that water was nearby, and that they could see clearly around them, right up to the rim that surrounded the valley. They felt very safe and secure.

Charlie was a bit concerned about food, but there were plenty of berries, and plump moths lay piled in heaps in the rock hollows. It was nearly dark before they had finished eating.

The evening was warm and they settled down in the soft grass tussocks above the spring. 'You know, Charlie,' said Rose, 'we shouldn't worry too much about shelter from the weather. Do you remember our family talking about a picture in a book they were reading — it was an Airedale curled up asleep somewhere in a country in the far north. He was covered in snow with just his nose poking out.'

'Mmm. . .' Charlie responded sleepily. 'I hope we don't get too much snow, though. Might make finding food a bit hard.'

Before long, however, both Airedales were sound asleep, content that for the present they were safe and warm, and not hungry.

Aaron and Emma watched them as they settled down. Despite feeling pleased that Charlie and Rose had so readily adapted to their new environment, and clearly felt at home, they knew that food would be the problem. Although they themselves did not require food, they knew they did not have the capacity to supply any for Charlie and Rose.

OOFING

A few days later, Aaron and Emma were having some fun rushing through (or 'oofing' as they used to call it) a herd of cattle, many of which roamed the plains in summer, and pretending to snap at their heels. Although there was no sound, the cattle sensed something amongst them, and galloped across the country with the two invisible tormentors playfully snapping at their heels. After a kilometre or so Aaron slowed and waited for Emma to return (because she always chased them further). They had a long, refreshing drink in a creek, before wending their way back towards the Play Grounds, where Charlie and Rose were now living.

Rose and Charlie often witnessed these mock cattle stampedes. They watched in puzzlement as hind legs were thrown into the air as if to ward off an attacker, but no matter how hard they looked, they could never see what disturbed the herd.

But this day, as they watched, they saw in the distance a fox trotting through the heathland, head held high and with what looked like a large hare in its mouth.

Normally (and he knew this from having tried) Charlie didn't attempt to intercept the hunter. He knew that the fox could outrun him easily. But this time, the fox seemed confused, running this way and that, jumping up above the bushes as if looking for something, turning back on itself; and all the time coming towards their grounds.

It seemed oblivious to their presence. Crouching low, Charlie crept quickly towards the hunter under the cover of the heath. Soon he was within twenty metres, and hearing the fox coming towards him, he leapt towards the unsuspecting animal.

The fox stopped, startled, ran a few metres to his left, then stopped suddenly and ran back to his right again. Charlie, not hindered by a hare, was able to keep right on his tail, and just as he drew beside the fox, it looked quickly sideways at him, dropped the hare and shot off in a hurry, disappearing over a rise.

Charlie stopped in his tracks, stunned at these events and wondering at his own powers of hunting. He retrieved the still warm hare, and trotted back to show Rose what they would have for supper tonight

... the fox shot off in a hurry, disappearing over a rise ...

instead of their usual harsh fare. She was delighted, thinking that, with pups on the way, a meal such as this every two or three days, supplemented by hard rations, would get her by.

As Aaron and Emma watched Charlie heading back to his mate with his 'catch', they laughed together, thinking how successful their spontaneous play had been in rounding up the fox. They had noticed on previous occasions that other foxes 'sensed' something when they were around and became uneasy.

'Well, now we know how to organise some meals for Charlie and Rose, don't we, Em?'

'Yes,' she said, 'and particularly with Rose having pups soon. She'll need plenty of meat.'

She watched Aaron's face as he realised that the arrival of a litter of pups could add to their responsibilities and need for vigilance. It was a challenge he viewed with both pleasure and concern, for he was in no doubt that dangers would exist for the pups in their wild environment.

PREGNANCY

There was little left of the hare when Charlie and especially Rose had finished.

'You're eating well Rose, you've probably had more than me, and you're still looking for scraps.'

'And so I should, Charlie. I'm not only feeding myself now, you know.'

'Know? Know what, Rose?' he said, rather bewildered.

'You're not very observant,' she said with a chuckle. 'Haven't you noticed that I'm putting on weight?'

Suddenly it dawned on Charlie just what Rose was saying. 'You mean . . . you mean you're going to have puppies?' he gasped.

The thought of becoming a father, even way out here in this wilderness, filled him with excitement. He bounded off, running flat out, cutting around bushes with his tail tucked in, passing Rose full pelt, and disappearing over a rise. In an ever-increasing curve, mouth open, ears back, he flashed behind a distant outcrop, and ran flat out until he was right in front of Rose again. He stopped dead and flopped on the ground with his tongue hanging out as he panted in great gusts.

Looking into his mate's calm, deep brown eyes, he said between pants, 'Just as well I've learned how to catch hares — you'll certainly need building up. I'll have to go out at sun-up every day and hunt until I catch something to eat.'

And that's just what he did. Next morning, as dawn painted the lightening sky with bands of deep pink, he left without waking Rose and set off with the sun behind his left shoulder. So too did Aaron and Emma; and they knew that this would become a regular ritual for them. Not that it mattered, because they didn't sleep very much. They just rested, not because they were tired, because they never were; they just liked to lie with eyes closed and dream their own dreams of the past.

Charlie wasn't sure which way he should be going, and as he sniffed around just about every rock and clump of bushes, he travelled neither fast nor far. The sun was casting long shadows across the plains and he could feel its warmth on his back. Suddenly a hare shot up from beneath his paws.

Startled, he hesitated a moment, by which time the hare was well away from him. But he knew before he started the chase that it was too fast for him, and after a few hundred metres he became confused by pathways of crossing scents.

He stopped to sniff, but there were too many strong smells. Charlie felt confused, as well as a bit disheartened. He wandered well into the afternoon, stopping to drink from pools or streams, and finding some small stranded trout which he ate, for he too was hungry.

He felt that he should be heading back to Rose and turned back towards the north-east, with the sun now behind him. Loping along, he covered a great distance. Suddenly, he saw a very large bird crouching on the ground ahead of him. A few days before, he and Rose had watched a pair of eagles circling high in the blue sky, and had seen them diving towards the ground, but he didn't recognise this as an eagle until he was very close. Barking, he ran towards it. The eagle took off into the air with a few short hops as Charlie approached, and circled about fifty metres overhead. Charlie saw that it had been feeding on the fresh carcass of an old wallaby, which had probably died from

Charlie and Rose had watched a pair of eagles circling high in the blue sky ...

natural causes the night before.

Oh, thought Charlie, this is great . . . at least I'll have something to take back to Rose. She must be so hungry by now.

Gripping the half-eaten carcass by the neck with his strong jaws, Charlie headed towards home. His instincts were accurate and an hour later, with a few stops to rest and drink, he saw familiar slopes and rocky outcrops. The eagle had followed him all the way, gliding in slow circles, hoping that this new and unfamiliar intruder, who had taken off with its meal, would tire and drop the carcass.

Aaron and Emma, who had stayed with Charlie all day during his search, knew how tired he was. But there was no way he would give up now. Unable to assist but knowing that Charlie was nearly back to Rose with his prize, they raced ahead to watch his return to his mate. Rose was sitting quietly near their cave, wondering where Charlie could be. She had eaten little today, mostly some sweet red berries picked from a matting plant, some daisy flower heads, and a few beetles and moths.

As Aaron looked at this handsome mother-to-be, he thought just how much a part of her surroundings she had become.

'It's easy for us,' said Emma, picking up Aaron's thoughts, 'we don't have to worry about food, but we know how difficult it will be for Rose when the pups are born.'

Thoughts of scavenging dingoes and foxes, and a hungry eagle, raced through Aaron's mind. We'll have to be on our guard all the time, he thought to himself.

Just then Rose stood up. She looked up towards the rim of the basin, and saw Charlie coming down the slope, the remains of the wallaby still firmly clasped in his jaws. Joyfully she bounded to meet him.

There was no doubting he was pleased with himself, she thought happily, but waited until he had dropped the food in front of their overhanging shelter.

'Now tell me!' she said. 'How was your day? You must be so tired. You've been gone for ages. However did you find this food?'

His story (even with a bit of embellishment of how he had to fight off the eagle) made her feel so proud of him. He cared so much about her. She had no doubt that she would be looked after and well fed over the weeks of her pregnancy, and afterwards, when the pups were born.

Charlie had learned a lot from that day, and now realised that there were signs by which he would be able to find food without always having to hunt himself. He became very attuned to reading the messages of the bush, and what birds, dingoes and foxes meant in the way of opportunities for acquiring food.

They were seldom short of some meat, whether a dead hare, wallaby or even a bird, and when he couldn't find any of these, in his wider travels Charlie picked mouthfuls of berries, which added some sweetness to the dry flavourless beetles.

And while all the pools had dried up, and the dead trout had long since been scavenged, he did have a fun game close to home chasing and catching grasshoppers, which were more nutritious than dried beetles and the now dry moths. Aaron and Emma were enthralled watching the development of Charlie's skills, and had no concerns for the health and fitness of Rose, who by now no longer joined Charlie on his travels. These days she only went with him to hunt grasshoppers and for a drink down at the creek.

RESTLESSNESS

One night, as he sat watching the starry sky wheel above him, Aaron felt again an urge that had been tugging at him for some time. With the new adventures that had filled his life during the past weeks, he had pushed these feelings into the back of his mind. But now that the security of Charlie and Rose seemed assured, the thoughts emerged again strongly.

'Em,' he said, 'would you mind if I went travelling for a while? I feel I want to visit some of our old places again, and p'raps see how Sue and Bill and Alice are.'

Emma had known he was restless. She had seen the faraway look in his eyes, but hadn't known what it meant.

'Of course not, Aaron, but how long would you be away?'

'Not long. I'd certainly be back well before the pups are born, say two weeks, no more. It's not as if I'm needed here for the present.'

He was thinking to himself that if he didn't go now, with the future responsibility of the pups, he might not get a chance for a very long time.

'Why don't you go first thing tomorrow, then you will be back with a week or so to spare before the pups are due.'

'Thank you, Emma. I don't like leaving you, but you won't be on your own, and you'll have plenty to keep you busy.'

Emma thought to herself that even without Charlie and Rose, she would never be lonely now in their spirit place, and she lay down again to think of coming events. Aaron did likewise, but he was thinking more of where he would go and who he might see.

At first light, after making sure that Charlie and Rose appeared secure, he said his farewells to Emma, touched her nose lovingly with his and, turning to the south-west, quickly disappeared. Emma watched him till he vanished and then turned her attention to the other two, judging what they would need for the coming events and then floating the ideas towards them.

'Rose,' said Charlie, 'I've been thinking that our shelter needs to be a bit bigger, perhaps deeper, so that you can take the pups further into the cave. This will give us better weather protection, and help if a dingo or fox gets the wrong idea.'

He saw by the look on her face that this last statement may have been a mistake. 'Not that I can't protect you from anything,' he added, only making Rose more concerned.

To cover his embarrassment, Charlie jumped up and started pacing out how much he would have to dig out, and planning what he would do with the soil. He soon had it worked out and as he explained his plan to her, he could see Rose's fears melting. It would take him the best part of three weeks to finish the work to his satisfaction, for he still had to provide food of course, and it would be a busy time.

Aaron didn't hurry his journey, and actually changed his direction, heading south-east rather than south-west. He and Emma, and later Alice, had spent many happy times with Sue and Bill in the far eastern forest lands of this country, exploring rivers by foot and canoe, travelling up inlets of lake systems by boat, and climbing to the tops of high mountains, where they would sit gazing at distant views through the clear air.

But he only stayed a short time in these lands. Although he saw people he knew and places where he had been happy with Sue and Bill, he knew he had an ultimate goal far to the west where he wanted to spend most of his time.

And so, at the end of the first week, he saw the familiar mountains and valleys close to his old home. These were the last of the high mountains where the snow lay, and as he looked down upon the twisted snow gums and springy heathlands he knew he was nearly home.

Suddenly a movement caught his eye. A lone figure was moving across the open plains. It looked like a dog, but certainly not a dingo, and it was much too big for a fox. Swooping lower, he was startled to see the shape and colour of the dog as it came into focus. By the aura of soft light around its body he could tell it was a spirit dog. And it was an Airedale.

AIRLIE

His mind raced. Was he lost, was he back on the high plains? He couldn't be.

'Emma? Is that you? It's me, Aaron . . . stop running.'

The other dog stopped, paw lifted in mid-flight, and when it turned around, Aaron realised it wasn't Emma.

'Who are you?' he asked gently as he quietly approached her. 'What are you doing here on your own?'

'Oh, you startled me. I wasn't expecting anyone else, let alone another Airedale. My name's Airlie, and I've been up here for many summers and winters. What's your name? Where have you come from?' she said, her eyes wide with surprise.

'My name is Aaron,' he replied, 'and I live with my sister on the great high plains far to the north-east. But why are you here on these plains? What brought you here? Is this your spirit place?'

'Yes,' she said slowly, and a little sadly. 'My family and I used to come here a lot; we walked lots, and collected and photographed plants, and the children, there were three of them, used to try and catch fish in the pools. I always felt at home here, even more so than in the great dry desert to the west or the forested mountains where we also used to go sometimes.'

'Are you lonely?' Aaron asked.

'Sometimes I am . . . but this is a very popular place in all seasons, so there's

'My name's Airlie, and I've been up here for many summers and winters ...'

plenty to see and do. I play with other dogs that come up here for trips like I used to, but of course they don't play back. I hope to see my family again sometime, but I never have . . . perhaps they don't come up here anymore.'

Aaron remembered that he and Emma and Sue and Bill had been up here a few times, but obviously their paths had never crossed.

'I have travelled away for short trips,' said Airlie. 'I even went back to our old home in the city but I didn't know anyone there, so I came back here. I'm all right . . . I'm used to it here.'

As day faded to night they sat and talked, each one recounting experiences and adventures, and Airlie was fascinated by the story of Charlie and Rose. But there were also aspects of Aaron's stories about his earlier life that revived memories for her, and made her heart race. She could not place the feeling. She was enjoying his company, and as he talked she studied the way he gazed into the distance, or moved his head to follow a flock of birds flying to their night roosting places.

And so the night passed, but Airlie's feelings of excitement remained. What was it? Was it having the company of another spirit . . . or something deeper?

'I was going on from here to visit my old home today,' said Aaron next morning, as they sat together watching the golden light touch the shining leaves on the old snow gums. 'Would you like to come with me? It would be a change for you, and company for me.'

'Yes, I think I would,' Airlie replied after a slight hesitation. After all, she hadn't travelled away from her country for many seasons. 'Yes, maybe I would like a change of scenery, perhaps a new adventure.'

And so they set off on their short journey southwards, little knowing that Airlie would not return to her high plains again.

Soon Aaron saw the fire tower on the tall hill that he knew, and below was the broad valley where he had lived. He felt a sense of excitement — it had been too long since he had left here to join Emma. He saw the billabong first, then the house, now partly hidden by the trees, so much bigger than when he had last seen them.

'There's my old home, Airlie, that's where Sue and Bill and Alice live . . . see, it's not far from where you've been living all this time.'

As they approached, a man emerged from the house, followed by two cavorting dogs, and going down to the edge of the billabong, he started throwing feed to the waterbirds.

Airlie was overcome by the strangest feelings.

'Who's that, Aaron?' she asked tremulously.

'That's Bill,' he replied joyously. 'And there's Alice . . . and that little chap, he must be new,' he added.

'But . . . but it's the same Bill that I loved and lost! I can't believe he was so close and I didn't know . . . I could have come here visiting too.'

They walked towards the group who were quietly feeding bread to groups of ducks and swamphens, all busily gathering a share of the food.

'Look at the puppy, the way he and Alice play; they both look very happy,' Airlie observed. 'I wonder what his name is?'

Just then the pup waddled into the lake to recover some bread missed by the birds.

'Hey, come on Aemon, you've had enough!' called Bill. 'Leave something for the birds!'

'Aemon, that's a good name,' Aaron said, 'Why does it sound familiar?'

Airlie had gone closer to Bill. She walked all around him to make sure she knew him.

'Yes . . . it's the same Bill, a bit different — his hair and beard are not the same colour but it's definitely the same one.'

A woman's voice called from the verandah and as Aaron bounded off, Airlie looked towards this new figure, uncertain who it was.

'I'll be up in a minute, Sue,' called Bill. 'We'll just have a game with the ball to get some of the energy out of these two!'

Sue, thought Airlie, still uncertain. I don't remember that name . . . but it must just be my memory, because Aaron knows who it is. Airlie did not know that Bill was no longer with his first family, the one she had belonged to, with the three children she had mentioned to Aaron.

Aaron had explained to her that Bill and Sue didn't have any children but that he and Emma had been their family — and then later Alice had joined the family, and now there was obviously another arrival, little Aemon.

HOME AGAIN

Aaron by this time had settled himself on a small deck at the front of the verandah, overlooking the lake. Airlie joined him, as Sue sat down beside them with a cup of tea. Aemon toddled over to her with the ball, and she threw it back towards the billabong so that he could chase it again. Bill joined Sue and they sat drinking their tea, little knowing that within a metre or so the two spirit Airedales were likewise sitting, gazing over the water at the birds splashing about on its sparkling surface.

As Aaron watched little Aemon chase the ball, he remembered how, when he was young, he and Bill had played almost every night, and was pleased that this tradition of fun and games continued.

'I spent a lot of time on this deck,' he remarked to Airlie, as she curled up beside him, 'particularly in my later years when I wasn't so active. Alice would sit with me sometimes, but she was very busy and if there were any cows next door she'd always want to go looking. This is where I went to sleep for the last time, and then I flew to find my darling Emma.'

As Aaron spoke, Airlie looked over her shoulder at Bill; his eyes had an old sadness about them. She had loved him very much, and was not to know that he still thought of and spoke about her often with Sue. He had never got over her disappearance, never knowing where she had gone and whether she may have been injured. She thought how foolish she had been, wandering out through an open gate on that fateful night, following scents and strange smells until she was lost.

She was many kilometres away from home and very hungry when she was picked up by an old man in his car, who could see she was lost. Even though she was only five at the time he called her 'old girl', and when they reached his home after a long drive his wife fed her and fussed over her.

The couple telephoned a lot of people and looked in a lot of papers, but she gathered they could not find where she had come from. She had not had her collar on (which had her name and address engraved on it) the day she became lost. The old couple called her 'Lady', and looked after her very well. They were

He saw the billabong first, then the house,
partly hidden by the trees ...

Aemon toddled over with the ball ...

kind and loving, and she remained with them for a long time until she became very tired and went to sleep. She remembered the old couple kneeling beside her, their arms about each other. Gently they stroked her ears and body, and their tears fell silently.

When her spirit left her body, she went in search of her original family. After a long time she found the house where she had lived but, as she had already told Aaron, her family had shifted. It was then that she started her big journey to find her spirit home.

'You'd like Emma.' Her own reverie was broken by Aaron's quiet murmur.

'I'm sorry, Aaron, I must have been dreaming. Does Alice look anything like her?'

'No, not really. Emma was bigger than Alice and she had a permanent smile on her face, especially when all her family was together. Come, I'll show you a picture.' And with this they stood up and walked through into the house and the big open living area.

'What a beautiful home, Aaron. No wonder you were so happy here. Just look at all the photographs of places you've been together,' said Airlie, as she gazed at the walls covered with framed pictures, mostly of the Airedales.

Airlie wandered around the big sunny room which had several windows looking out onto the billabong. She stopped to look at a collection of pictures of Aaron. She saw him as a baby puppy, then as a handsome youngster sitting proudly with head held high. And there was even one of him and Alice in party hats with a cake with one, two, three, four . . . eleven candles on it. Aaron looked as if he could hardly resist the temptation to gobble down the whole cake.

There were many other pictures of him, on his own in remote beautiful places, serene and at peace. Others were with Alice and Sue or Bill, in the bush and by the billabong. On one wall was a set of three big pictures of Aaron with Emma, glowing with all the love they shared.

Yes, Emma did smile. As she remembered Aaron's story of how Bill had found her, hungry, and very dirty, and brought her home to start a new life, Airlie understood the smile.

The days went quickly. Aaron and Airlie followed Alice and Aemon as they galloped around the billabong every morning, or went walking in the hills behind the property with Bill and Sue. At night they would come inside and listen to family talk and were comforted by the warmth and love which surrounded them.

'I'm happy for you that you had such a loving family, Aaron, but I also feel sad that I lost my first love.' Airlie spoke quietly. 'But aren't I lucky that at least I've found Bill again and we can visit at any time?'

'Of course, Airlie. It helps, doesn't it?' replied Aaron gently.

A few days later they were sitting on the deck watching the daylight fade, when Aaron spoke. Mostly he had been quiet during the time they had spent here, but now she knew what he was about to say. 'I'm going to have to leave soon, Airlie. I must get back to the great high plains well before Rose's puppies are born. I've got to make sure Emma's all right and that Charlie has finished getting things ready. Do you want to stay here for a while more or will you go back to your plains? I could go with you . . . it's on my way.'

Airlie had given deep thought to this very question over the past days. She had never considered that she would do other than wander across her country alone forever. Turning to look at Aaron, she said, 'Would you — do you think that I could spend some time with you and Emma on the great high plains — just for a little while? I wouldn't stay long, then I could go home.'

She thought the expression on his face softened, and there was a new light in his eyes as he turned to face her. He didn't speak for a few moments, then said very simply, 'We'd love to have you visit us, Airlie, for as long as you wish. I could use another set of female paws when the puppies are due.' He said this with a laugh in his voice and a twinkle in his eyes. Her heart lifted, and happiness enveloped her.

'Oh, thank you Aaron. That's very generous of you. I didn't want to impose on you and Emma, but I do so want to meet her and see where you live; and of course I would help with Rose and the puppies.'

Together they sat in the soft evening light, watching the swallows hawking for insects over the water. It was their last night with Sue and Bill, and Alice and Aemon.

RETURNING

With the dawning of the new day, before anyone was awake, they started their journey. Alice awoke and sat up as they silently left the house. She barked, but didn't know what had disturbed her, for there was nothing to see.

They took two days to complete the return trip. Airlie wanted to pass over her home plains, where she had spent so many seasons. It seemed remote and lonely as she looked down upon it. As they passed beyond it, she felt a sense of excitement, a feeling she hadn't known since she was young, a great sense of anticipation. Would Emma accept her? she asked herself, immediately chastising herself for prejudging what might happen.

The night found them settled in a grassy hollow at the edge of a forest, where a clear spring sparkled from a group of rocks. They drank and settled down comfortably, talking about what they had seen during their days of travelling, but each thinking to themselves of what tomorrow would bring.

As dawn broke, the night mist lifted and the new day's sun started its journey; but all that Airlie could see was a solid darkness with a capping of bright light behind it. As the light became more intense the darkness took shape; trees and rocks were outlined, valleys and ridges more defined. Airlie gasped. They seemed to go up and up for ever.

'That's the great high plains,' said Aaron, 'that is where we live and roam. Emma and I still haven't seen all of it, and we probably never will. The only road across it is very steep and rough, and that must have been where Charlie and Rose became lost.'

Airlie was overcome by the scale of this wilderness, as they started the final stage of their journey.

About this time Charlie had woken and come to the entrance to their cave, which was proving dry and warm. They had had heavy rain on a number of occasions but none had got past the high bank he had built at the entrance.

Emma watched him emerge and stretch, then mark his territory anew as he looked to see what the weather would be. Each of them was also thinking about

Rose, who was within days of whelping, as her swelling nipples indicated. Charlie's thoughts were on finding food and keeping an eye out for predators which might wander into the region. Emma was thinking of Aaron's promise to be 'back in time'. She knew she could handle anything that came up, such as a nosy fox or even a hawk drawn to the smells of whelping, but she would be happier if he were here too.

She rose and walked over to drink at the stream. She was thirsty, and her spirit needed refreshing. As she lapped, the broken surface of the water suddenly reflected a new image, or was it two images? The surface flattened as she ceased drinking, and there, reflected in the water, was Aaron. But not on his own. Surprised, she lifted her head and he smiled at her.

'Hello, Emma. I hope I'm back in time?' Aaron spoke softly.

She looked from one to the other, a bit startled to see another Airedale, obviously female, and obviously shy, as she stood slightly back from Aaron. Overcoming her surprise, Emma bounded to her soul mate and they touched noses, not once but three times.

'Oh Aaron, I'm so glad you're back! You don't know how happy I am to see you. I think the puppies will be born very soon,' she said quickly.

'Emma, this is Airlie,' said Aaron, 'and she'll be staying with us for a little while. We've lots to tell you, specially about seeing Sue and Bill and Alice.'

If Emma felt uncomfortable initially about this newcomer, her uneasiness disappeared and changed to excitement as Aaron, with occasional shy interruptions or corrections from Airlie, told her the complete story of his travels. Emma felt twinges of sadness as he recounted the time spent with Sue, Bill and Alice, and images of the home that she too had loved so much came back to her.

'. . . and the new pup Aemon . . . Alice and he are very happy, running and wrestling, sniffing out new smells and playing all their games. Aemon's a nice name, and familiar, but I can't work out why.'

'How do you spell it?' asked Emma.

'Oh, I think it's A-E-M-O-N,' replied Aaron.

Emma thought for a moment. 'You're a duffer, Aaron, fancy you not being able to work it out, you're usually the clever one around here.'

‘What do you mean?’ he said with a puzzled look on his face.

‘Aemon,’ she said, ‘It’s an anu — ana-something — anagram, that’s it, of parts of our two names. Emma and Aaron.’

‘Of course,’ Aaron said, ‘how clever of you. I’m slipping up in my old age.’

They all smiled, now feeling relaxed in each other’s company.

Airlie, who had contributed little to the conversation, sat absorbing the scale of this wild and beautiful place. She watched Charlie and Rose come to the creek for a drink, and looking at how big Rose had grown, she thought that they hadn’t arrived back a day too soon. Now she glanced from Emma to Aaron, understanding the loving bond which existed between these two. Could she be part of it? Even for a short time?

Aaron arose, and went to inspect the renovated cave, looking with approval at the bank which Charlie had built across the opening. It formed a narrow passage, making it a squeeze for anything large going in or out.

Good defence strategy, Charlie, he mused, and he thought about where he, Emma and Airlie would take up their new resting spots close to the cave. He had already discussed with Airlie some of the problems the new parents and their litter might have from predators, and they had devised spooking strategies to frighten them off.

The following days were spent talking and waiting, which gave Emma and Airlie plenty of time to get to know one another well. Their bond grew strongly over this time.

BIRTH

Charlie spent his time collecting a store of berries and beetles and grasshoppers, putting them onto a shelf he cleared in the back of the cave. And while he heard both dingoes and foxes calling on far plains and ridges, for the present all was quiet in their little valley. Still, he would maintain a constant vigil. Instincts, long buried within town-bred dogs, had surfaced over the past weeks, and Charlie had developed a toughness of both body and mind.

Returning at mid-morning with a hare scavenged from a gang of ravens, he was greeted by a strange new smell. Who was here, he wondered?

He looked around, but saw no sign of an intruder. The invisible trio positioned around the cave knew more than Charlie did, and exchanged knowing smiles.

With the hare still in his jaws, he cautiously moved to the entrance of the cave where the new scent was at its strongest. His eyes took a few moments to adjust to the gloom, and then he saw Rose lying on her side apparently licking something which lay against her breast.

She looked up at Charlie. 'Look, the first one is born. I'm just cleaning him up. The next one is due any minute.'

Charlie was elated, but knowing that a male Airedale played no part in the whelping of the puppies he had fathered, he said, 'I'll just wait outside, Rose . . . call me if you're hungry or thirsty, I could bring you some wet moss to lick.' With this he moved back to sit some distance from the cave.

Rose, very occupied with the whelping,

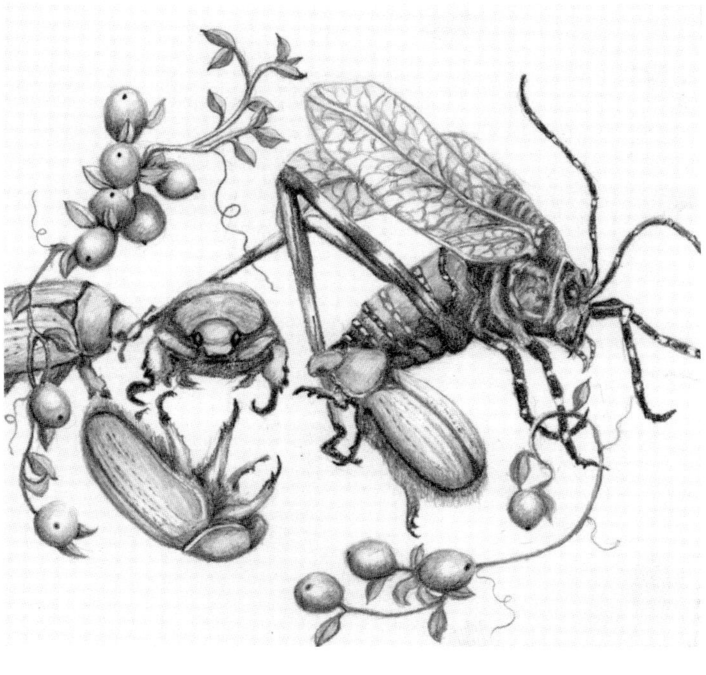

Charlie spent his time collecting a store of berries and beetles ...

still managed a smile at the concern Charlie showed for her welfare.

There were four puppies in all, two male, two female. Rose remembered that she had been one of a litter of ten, and guessed that their harsh, sometimes meagre diet had dictated how many puppies she would have. She lay with the now washed quartet contentedly drinking from her ample nipples. 'Charlie, come and see your family,' she called to him. It was nearly dark, but he could just make out the four tiny bodies lined up at Rose's tummy.

'Are you all right, Rose?' he asked anxiously.

'I'm tired and very thirsty. Could you bring me some moss?' she said, her dark eyes gazing at him lovingly.

'Of course. Are you hungry? I've got some food here for you,' he added.

'No, not at the moment, just very dry in my mouth,' she replied.

He hurried to the creek, and biting off a large piece of moss he soaked it in the refreshing water, then quickly re-entering the cave, he placed it in a depression in a rock near Rose's head. He withdrew immediately, because he knew how protective mothers were of their puppies. This stage was not part of his role.

And so for two days he replenished the water and brought food for Rose. On the third day, she decided to stretch her legs and go quickly to the stream for a long refreshing drink.

Instinctively Charlie positioned himself at the entrance to the cave until she returned.

Charlie's daily patterns now changed dramatically. He only spent a little time with Rose who, as nature determines, became very protective of her litter, excluding even her mate from close contact with them. He roamed far and wide for food to keep Rose's strength up now that she had four extra mouths to feed, and his new cunning ensured that there was always 'food on the table', or at least at the mouth of the cave.

Before he left for any food-gathering trips, he placed a number of wet mosses in a depression in the rock outside the cave, which did hold water when it rained. So even if he was late back Rose would never be without water.

Often Airlie would follow him on a trip, learning about this vast new world she had come to, so much bigger and higher than the one where she had lived for so long.

He placed a number of wet mosses in a depression in the rock outside the cave ...

She was enjoying the companionship and the long talks with Aaron and Emma, and she loved peeping into the cave to watch the growth of the puppies. One morning, when Charlie had been gone for some time, the three of them were sitting quietly together when Aaron sprang up, his head turning from side to side, looking and sensing.

'What is it?' said Emma quickly, 'What startled you?'

He didn't reply, for he hardly needed to. A large male dingo had appeared on the rim of their valley, clearly visible against the sky.

They were all standing by now. This was a real threat to the puppies' safety. The dingo was sniffing the air and looking in their direction, feeling rather than seeing another presence.

Slowly he moved down the slope, following scent tracks, wary of Charlie's recent smells and territory markings. He was a big dog in the prime of life and very strong.

Reaching the entrance to the dark cave, he inserted his muzzle into the narrow space above Charlie's earth barrier. The smell of young puppies and a lactating mother was strong.

Suddenly he leapt back with a howl, his paw rubbing at his face. Rose had fastened her teeth into his nose and had drawn blood. The pain soon abated and, as he sensed an easy breakfast, he again approached the narrow entrance to the cave. Rose had by now pushed the pups to the very back of the cave, and she was crouched, teeth bared, inside the entrance. She would fight to the death for the pups.

As the dingo reached the entrance again, he was faced with bared teeth and a constant menacing growl. Suddenly he sensed another presence and spun around. There was nothing there. But now it was behind him, now to one side, then annoying his legs.

He hopped and jumped around as if attacked by a swarm of bees, but could see nothing. He was spooked and this of course was what his three invisible tormentors intended. He was still close to the entrance to the cave, and his right leg presented an easy target for a quick snap from Rose, who then immediately withdrew, still growling ferociously.

Again he thrust his broad head into the opening, scrabbling at the dirt mound in an effort to clear more space so he could easily enter the cave. Rose charged at him, totally heedless of her own safety, and locked powerful jaws on his nose and upper lip. She applied fearsome pressure; she heard teeth snapping and blood entered her mouth. And while she hung on remorselessly, the unseen tormentors were still busy outside the cave. With the dingo in Rose's vice-like grip, he was unable to ward off this constant bombardment. Eventually, driven now by his own fear, he wrenched free from Rose and, with blood streaming from his mouth, ran up the slope and disappeared over the rim, the tormentors still in pursuit.

A short distance away Charlie, who had found a discarded hare not too far beyond the valley rim, was returning to Rose and the puppies, when he saw a dingo acting very strangely as it fled across his path some fifty metres away. He could see that it was running very fast but every ten metres or so it would turn back, snapping at the air, then run for some distance and repeat the performance, first one side then the other.

It must have bees after it, thought Charlie. But then he realised that it had come from the direction of the camp, and he ran. His heart was in his mouth at the thought of Rose's danger.

In the meantime the trio followed the dingo, harassing him all the way until he disappeared down a long valley into heavy timber. Then they returned to camp, well satisfied with their efforts.

Charlie rushed over the rim and down the slope, calling for Rose, anxious to hear her response. 'I'm here Charlie, up by the stream, I'm having a wash and a drink,' she called.

Quickly he rushed to her side.

'Blood! Where did that come from? Not from any of the puppies? Or you?' he asked with fear in his voice.

'No, they're all right and so am I, but I'm not sure the dingo is,' she said. And she told him the story of the attack and how she had repelled the hunter. His heart swelled with pride as his beautiful partner told her story, and he helped her finish washing, licking clean the parts she could not reach. She was not injured, he noted with relief. Together they went back to the cave and ate the meal that he had brought.

'I don't suppose a dingo's ever encountered an Airedale before, especially one with puppies to protect,' Charlie commented, when they had finished eating.

'No, he seemed surprised at how I just hung on, but it was strange, Charlie, I didn't feel that I was fighting him on my own,' Rose said. 'I can't explain it but something seemed to be attacking him from all sides . . . it was a bit spooky, and I think he was running away from that as much as from me.'

'Mmm . . . I don't think by the way he was acting that he'll bother us again,' Charlie said.

He was right. Neither the dingo nor any other predators came near them. Foxes and dingoes gave the region a wide berth, and a few weeks later, when the puppies were exploring the valley for the first time and testing out their legs, a circling eagle moved to another hunting ground after one glance. The word had obviously got around.

Rose would fight to the death for the pups ...

PUPPIES

The puppies grew very quickly, played often and slept soundly, giving both parents and their unseen guardians great pleasure, even though none of the invisible three had ever been parents themselves. Summer was nearly over and the nights were becoming very cold. The winds came now more regularly from the south-west; it was mid-April, and winter was not far away.

The puppies were becoming very adventurous, exploring the country around their little home, but always with one or both of their parents. Late one day, they sat together on the rim of their valley and watched a storm far to the south on distant hills. Even though Charlie and Rose could see that there was much thunder and lightning, its sound was very muted and didn't really worry them. Sometime late in the night, Charlie awoke with the faint smell of smoke in his nostrils, and went up to the rim to investigate. He looked southward and could see small patches of fire where they had seen lightning earlier. Returning to the entrance to the cave where he now

Baby Aaron

Baby Emma

mostly rested, he put Rose's fears to rest about any possible danger. They went back to sleep again until dawn bathed the basin with smoky light.

It was a morning ritual for the six of them to walk (or run, roll and gambol in the case of the pups) to a stream for their first drink, noting new scents on the ground and bushes left by animals who had passed through in the night. Charlie noted that while wombats, mice, wallaby and insect smells were numerous, there was never any sign of other dogs.

Rose was enjoying mothering her brood, proud of how fast they were growing, and their joy of life. One male and one female were much bigger than the other two. The littlest one of all was the second female. This did not stop her being in everything, biting at tails and ears constantly, barking or growling as she did so. Because she was so active and noisy Rose had called her Storm, and she was her dad's favourite, even though she was all over him when he tried to rest. When he tired of her hyperactivity, his low growl was warning enough to back off.

The smallest male Rose had called Wind, because that was how he ran, like the wind, always the first of the four by a long way in any race. She hadn't yet given names to the other two, the one so big

Rose was enjoying mothering her brood, proud of how fast they were growing, and their joy of life ...

and sober, always watching over the two smaller ones, while his sister was gentle and still, both of them often sitting quietly, watching, while Storm and Wind exhausted themselves with constant activities. It's strange though, thought Rose, when I see them sitting there side by side, two names keep coming into my head, but from where I just don't know.

One of these names was 'Aaron', strong and masculine; 'Emma' was the other name, and certainly suited her gentle girl. The more she thought of these names, the more she thought how suitable they were. And that's what they became, much to the surprise of the older invisible Aaron and Emma.

But it was no surprise to Airlie. She had thought how alike, in their puppy stage, the new arrivals were to Aaron and Emma. She had thought about it so long and with such concentration, even calling the puppies by these names to herself, that Rose had picked up her thought messages.

It was confusing for a few days, but soon the older pair stopped responding when either Charlie or Rose called, 'Come on Aaron, come on Emma, time for a rest.' They even felt a sense of pleasure in having their names given to this strong but gentle little pair.

Smoke was still wafting over them from the distant fires, borne by the winds from the ranges and valleys. One day, while they were all wandering some way from the basin, teaching the puppies how to pick up small berries in their teeth, Charlie lifted his head to a strange sound coming from the direction of the fires. At first he could see nothing. Then he saw a small dot gradually becoming larger. The noise grew as the thing approached them, low in the sky. Then it was above them and the sudden sound so close put fear into all of them. They scattered in all directions, but then, at Charlie's insistent barking, they ran together back towards their camp.

Having passed above them, the aeroplane turned. Previously, they had only ever seen these big silver birds very high in the sky, the noise a distant roar. Back came the plane, even lower than before, dipping a wing, just as the six dropped over the rim of the basin and headed for their cave.

While Rose ushered the puppies to safety, Charlie stopped and watched the flight of the plane as it turned again and made a final low pass over the basin before heading northward.

Disturbed by the noise and closeness of the plane, Aaron and Emma and Airlie were on the alert too, concerned for the safety of the Airedale family.

'That's the fire-spotter plane,' Aaron said to Emma and Airlie. 'We've seen it often, but because there haven't been any close fires this year, that's the first time it's been over here this summer.'

'Do you think it saw and recognised the family?' Emma asked.

'I'm sure it saw them, otherwise it wouldn't have kept coming back, but I don't know whether it knew who they were. It might have thought it was a family of dingoes,' Aaron replied.

When she realised that the noisy aeroplane was unlikely to return, Rose allowed the puppies out again, and Storm and Wind had a lot of pent-up energy to release after being confined to the cave for so long. Charlie, who had been gazing southward beyond the smoke haze, noted a great bank of dark grey cloud stretching as far as the eye could see.

'That could be a big storm approaching, Rose. I had better hunt up some food, in case it's a long one. If it comes while I'm away, make sure you and the family are safely in the cave. I might be away quite a while,' he warned.

They touched noses in farewell, and he loped up the side of the basin and over the rim. Wind thought that this was a game and went to follow his father.

'Not now,' Rose said, 'you can go hunting with your father when you're a bit bigger.'

Wind looked disappointed, but eventually returned to playing with Storm.

FIRST SNOW

Charlie headed towards the approaching grey clouds, which seemed to fill the southern sky. Moving swiftly and keeping his eyes and ears alert for signs of possible food he travelled south-west, where the bigger trees grew and where once before he had found a wallaby carcass.

But even though he was out for most of the day, it was not until he was on the homeward journey, with the ominous sky now hanging above him, that he managed to scrounge the leftover carcass of a hare from a group of ravens. The temperature was falling quickly and although it was not raining it was very cold. He turned for home with his meagre catch. The air was very still, which gave the great bank of cloud, motionless above him, an even more oppressive look. It was something new in his experience on the great high plains, and he wasn't sure what it meant.

The hungry puppies gnawed at the carcass of the hare after Rose and then Charlie had eaten a little of the meat each. This was supplemented by some beetles and grasshoppers that Rose had collected while he was away. The family went to the stream for a final drink before bedding down. The sky was very dark, even though it was not yet sunset. There was no wind, and a great silence lay across their little valley.

Charlie awoke much later feeling as if he were lightly covered in something cold. As he moved his head, the snow which had fallen silently while he slept scattered from his fur. He looked down at his feet. His front legs were almost covered, and as he looked over his shoulder, to check the entrance to the cave, he saw his back was covered with snow.

He hardly recognised the cave entrance. The mound at the front was white, as were the rocks above, and the floor of the basin was no longer grass and low shrubs, but a white carpet.

Standing up, he shook the snow from his coat. Without its usual summer trim, his fur was thicker than normal and insulated him well against the cold. Looking into the cave he saw that Rose and the pups were in a deep sleep, and decided not to disturb them. Instead he headed off into the new dawn light, with the snow still falling silently around and on him. When he retraced his steps some hours later with a mouthful of berries collected down at the edge of the tall forest, the snow had all but obliterated his footprints.

Four hungry puppies awaited him. They had already ventured from the cave to discover a new white world at their feet. The berries did not go far between them, and now this early snow covered the grass where Charlie may have found grasshoppers and beetles.

What was he to do? he thought to himself. Rose was worried, too.

'I'll just have to keep going back below the snowline and collect whatever I can,' he told her, with more confidence than he really felt.

Over the next two days, with snow falling only intermittently, and the occasional warm spell, the depth of the snow hardly increased, but it was still enough to make food hard to find. Charlie scraped away the snow in places where he knew berries might still be, and managed to gather a few. The puppies voiced their hunger often, and with rumbling stomachs they even found sleep difficult. And Rose, because of the tough diet, was not able to contribute anything to their diet, as her milk supply had dried up some days ago.

Charlie made up his mind to go further than he had before, and told Rose what he intended doing. 'I may well be away over-night if I don't find anything close, so that means that you'll have to scrounge what-ever berries and insects you can find on the bare patches of grass.'

Rose was not happy in the knowledge that he would be away for such a time, not only because of the puppies' hunger, but because she feared for him. Having given all the food to her and the four babies she knew he was tired and not his strongest.

But he left the next day, farewelling his family with parting touches of noses and licks to the puppies' heads. 'Try not to worry, Rose,' he said calmly. 'I'll be careful, and I'll be back as soon as I can.'

SPOTTED

At about this time Alan Hardy, the pilot of the aeroplane, was driving to the District Forest Office at Warramata to file his report on fire conditions. He was grounded due to the snow, which in any case had doused any fires within the alpine region. Just as he was about to leave the office he remembered the two dogs with four pups he'd seen way up on the remote high plains. He turned back to the officer, Merv Lane.

'Saw an unusual thing three days ago, Merv,' he commented, 'way up on that big depression area. Two adult dogs and four pups. When I first saw them I thought dingoes, but the colour was wrong so I went back twice at lower levels, and sure enough they weren't dingoes.'

'Not foxes?' asked Merv.

'No, too big; quite woolly — and they seemed, at least the adults did, to be black and tan; big dogs, strong looking. The pups were mostly black.'

'Do you think they could have been terriers, Alan?'

'I'm not sure, they could have been. Do you have any pictures?'

'Sure,' said Merv. 'I'll get the book the local vet lent to us. The kids want a dog, and he said that this is often the best way to pick one.'

Scanning down the page of terrier photos, Alan stopped at the Airedale. But as this showed a trimmed dog, it was hard to equate it with the woolly pair he'd seen running up on the high plains.

'Strange you picked an Airedale,' said Merv, 'even though you're not sure, because a pair escaped from a vehicle on the Middle Bluff road during a storm. It must have been, oh, sometime in November. The owners searched for two days and then came in here and reported them lost. They'd left them in the vehicle, but they got out somehow during a fierce thunderstorm. I've still got their address and phone number — I'll ring them.'

'What about the pups?' asked Alan. 'There were four of them, and they looked about two or three months old.'

'Yes, I'd better check with the owners if the dogs were neutered or not, and you'd better mark the spot on this map where you saw them.' Merv pushed the map across to Alan, who marked with a pencil

Alan marked with a pencil the site where he'd seen the dogs ...

the site where he'd seen the dogs.

'Mmm . . .' said Merv. 'Could be, I suppose, though that's a fair way from the road where they were lost.'

That night, Merv spoke with Mr Waters, who confirmed that yes, they had intended breeding with Charlie and Rose. In fact, they had already suspected that Rose might be pregnant, and were planning to have her tested on their return. It had added to their concerns about their much loved lost pair.

They hardly dared to think that their beautiful Airedales might be safe, and were concerned to hear of the snow. Merv said he would fax the map to them immediately with Alan's marks on it, and Mr Waters said that they would leave on Friday, two days away, as soon as the children had finished school.

'If you're going to camp overnight, be prepared for snow and low temperatures,' warned Merv. 'The forecast is for light snow, so please go prepared.'

They promised to do so.

HUNGER

It was the end of the first day and, tired and hungry, Charlie had travelled much further than ever before. His route had taken him into open forest, with the steep bluff of the high country always on his left. He had eaten little and drunk a lot of water, even if only to make his stomach feel full. Eventually he had a meal of berries, which were plentiful, and some grasshoppers, which weren't. The snows had driven them away, even from here where it lay only thinly.

Exhausted, he lay down beneath the low branches of a snow gum, with his back tucked against a large rock, and was instantly asleep. He awoke at first light, drank deeply at a nearby stream and continued his journey, thinking all the time of Rose and their family. He would have to find something soon or turn back. He was surprised how quickly the birds and most animals had moved to lower altitudes, well below where he was, when the snows began.

Emerging from the trees, he found himself in an open grassed area, in the middle of which was an old wooden hut. It seemed deserted. There was no smell of fresh smoke from the chimney, nor human scents on the ground around it.

The door, which was only lightly latched, showed a fair gap between it and the jamb. Sensing the possibility of food inside, Charlie inserted his broad muzzle into the gap and pushed. Nothing happened. Pulling back his head, he brought the door to, jamming his snout; this caused him to lift his head sharply in an attempt to free himself, and as he did so the latch slipped its catch. He pushed again, forcing the door to open suddenly, and tumbled inside.

Standing up and shaking himself, he started a search of the hut, which was very clean. He could see a number of tins on a high shelf, but from past failed attempts at trying to open tins with his teeth, they could just as well have been on the ground. His nose twitched at a strong smell of bread or biscuit, but he couldn't see anything. A rat scurried across a rafter and as he looked up at it, his eyes alighted on a heavy cotton bag, hanging by a rope from the rafter. It was directly above a table and well out of the reach of rats from both directions.

The rope even had an old tin lid inserted halfway up, so that rats could not come down it to the bag.

The table was not high and Charlie jumped onto it, easily bringing his nose in line with the bag. It was very full and definitely contained the smell. Charlie had found food, and a lot of it. But how to get it down was another thing, let alone how to take it back to camp. The neck was well tied and he didn't think it wise to rip the bag.

This left the option of gnawing through the rope, which at least would give him something to hang onto to carry his find home. A chair had been placed on the table and, resting his paws on its back, he started chewing the rope.

Back at their camp, Rose and the puppies were making a good job of finding little bits of food, even if it took them most of the day. They dug for beetles and sniffed under logs for moths, and at one stage a number of migrant grasshoppers came their way, and the pups, with much jumping about, were able to catch quite a few.

The silent three were not able to assist greatly, as there was little to spook (although Emma claimed that she had driven the grasshoppers in the right direction when she had run down the slope, playing invisibly with the pups). Aaron knew everything depended on Charlie's hunting skills, and that if further heavy snow came the puppies were unlikely to survive up here. They would all have to go down below the snow-line where some food might be found. Whether Charlie and Rose had thought of this possibility, he wasn't sure, and if they had, they would also have taken into account the dangers from dingoes or foxes in any new territory.

The rope parted after much gnawing and the bag hit the table with a heavy thud. Evidently some of what was in it had broken, but as nothing leaked onto the table, Charlie assumed that it was dry and probably chewable. It certainly smelt all right. Picking up the bag by the neck, he tested its weight. It was heavy, but not too heavy. Jumping down from the table, he headed out the door and started his return journey. He could tell it was not going to be easy, for his load dragged on the ground, and caught on roots and sticks.

Charlie repositioned his grip in the middle of the bag and it now hung evenly on both sides of his jaw ...

Realising that this might rip the bag, he repositioned his grip in the middle and it now hung evenly on both sides of his jaw. When it touched the ground, he knew it was time for a rest and a drink. His neck muscles ached with the strain.

Going directly home to Rose and the family would actually be quicker than his outward journey, when he had zigzagged across so much ground looking for food. Very tired, but still moving strongly, he arrived back at the Play Grounds in the late afternoon, much to the relief of Aaron, Emma and Airlie who saw him coming from some distance, and to Rose who saw that he was unharmed and had at least found something, even if she couldn't see what it was.

She ran to meet him, overjoyed at his return.

Dropping the bag at her feet, he greeted her in the traditional way, and responded to the joyful leaps and yaps of the puppies.

'I don't know what I've brought, Rose, but it smells fine and there's enough here, with the other bits and pieces we find, to last us perhaps for a week.'

'Oh Charlie,' she said, 'you are wonderful. You must be so tired and hungry yourself.'

Holding the cotton bag with a paw, he fastened his teeth into it and easily ripped a hole big enough to put his snout in. When he removed it he had a thick savoury biscuit in his mouth, which he bit into pieces. He gave one to each pup and gave a large piece to Rose. Only when they were chewing contentedly did he start eating one himself.

These were known as 'bush biscuits' and were high in protein and carbohydrates. They had probably been left by bushwalkers who intended returning to the hut sometime. One biscuit and a drink was both filling and a high source of energy; and the calcium was essential for the puppies' bones and teeth.

Charlie rested for the next two days, regaining his strength with regular food. He didn't think too much about the future when this food supply would run out. Towards the end of the week the snow started again and by Saturday night a heavy layer covered the ground. They were now halfway through the biscuits and the new snow meant that further food would be hard to find. Charlie knew that he would not find another hut with a food supply in it; they would have to ration out what they had.

A JOYFUL MEETING

Late that Friday, the Waters family arrived at the point where Charlie and Rose had disappeared nearly five months ago. They set up camp by the Landrover, and were soon in their sleeping-bags. Very early on Saturday morning, they set out for the point marked on the map which Merv had sent them.

It appeared to be a walk of about fifteen kilometres, so they knew that, with snow on the ground, it would take them more than one day. Initially they had been uncertain about the two children accompanying them, but as they were twelve and fourteen and both very used to carrying backpacks, they were allowed to come. But as Merv had said, however, that there might be a light snowfall, they went prepared.

In spite of the snow they covered about twelve kilometres on the first day. They all slept warmly in one tent, set up in a group of snow gums. After an early breakfast on Sunday morning, they set off again.

It was a bright morning, with just a few broken clouds drifting slowly across the early autumn sky. Charlie, Rose and the pups were having a drink at the creek, the babies splashing happily amongst the shiny pebbles and trying to catch the sparkling drops of water. In a moment of silence, they heard voices calling from afar. Charlie and Rose looked up simultaneously, gazing into the east across the vast plains. They could not see anything. Perhaps they had imagined it.

Turning, they called the puppies and set off back to their cave. But there were the voices again. Charlie and Rose stopped in their tracks — surely the voices were familiar? Standing like statues, their gaze fixed on the rim of their valley, they waited. There it was again, and in the distance they glimpsed movement, and saw a small group moving towards them, clearer now, like the calls.

'Rose . . . I think I know those voices.' Charlie's voice was uncertain.

'Oh, Charlie . . . you could be right. Do you really think it's them?' said Rose, a slight tremor in her reply.

The group was within a few hundred metres now, their voices very distinct.

It *is* them! Charlie thought, and let out

Charlie advanced a little way towards the people ...

a sharp deep bark, then another. Rose barked too.

They barked again, and the voices called louder, the group now breaking into as much of a trot as their backpacks would allow.

The puppies, uncertain about these strange new arrivals and perplexed by all the barking and calling, sat close together by Rose. Charlie advanced a little way towards the people. He was certain now, his tail wagging furiously as he barked more happy greetings. Rose followed him, wagging her tail just as fast. The puppies now scampered behind, Wind of course well in front of the roly-poly group.

The reunion was a mix of barking, laughing, rolling in the snow, tight hugs, licks and tears, and the puppies soon forgot their uncertainty and joined in.

Aaron, Emma and Airlie thought that they would join in the fun too, and scampered and rolled in the snow amongst the people and the Airedale family. After all, they'd been such a part of Charlie and Rose's life for so long that they all shared the happiness of this unexpected meeting.

When everyone had calmed down a little and every pup had been cuddled a dozen times and licked every face many more times, Mr Waters said, 'Well, this is where you've been, you two . . . and look what you've produced, you clever girl, Rose.'

Rose beamed proudly, her eyes sparkling as she looked at her brood.

'Show us where you've been living all this time, Charlie,' said Mr Waters. 'You look fit enough, even if you are a bit thin.'

Together they walked back to the rocky outcrop, led proudly by Charlie. The family all lay on their stomachs to look into the cave, where signs of long-term occupancy were evident.

'What's this, Dad?' asked young Peter as he reached into the cave and pulled out the cotton bag, now with only about a dozen biscuits left in it.

'Where did you get this from, Charlie?' asked Mr Waters. 'Judging by the bit of rope it looks like it's come from a hut somewhere. Aren't you a smart fellow, finding food for your family like this?'

Of course, the family would never know all the rest of the bush survival skills Charlie and Rose had developed. But they guessed the Airedales must have shown a lot of initiative, particularly with puppies on the way.

FAREWELLS

Rose and Charlie had not felt as relaxed or truly contented for a long time, and a sense of belonging overwhelmed them as they watched the children romping through the shallow snow with the puppies. The rest of the day passed quickly with exploring and play, *and* a meal of dried beef strips which all six Airedales spent much time chewing.

In the late afternoon, the Waters set their tent up a little distance from the rocky outcrop, and cleared away some snow so they could light a small fire. While the family sat around eating their dinner, Charlie, Rose and the puppies ate half of the bush biscuits, saving the other half for the trip out to the vehicle tomorrow.

By eight o'clock the Waters were ready for bed and, giving all six Airedales a big hug, they retired to their tent. The puppies, tired from their day's excitement, climbed down into their cave not long afterwards, and were soon cuddled up together, fast asleep.

The night was clear and crisp and the full moon bathed the snow with a silver lustre. Charlie and Rose slowly walked up to the rim of the valley, and sat side by side, their shoulders touching. They could see for a great distance and even spied a lone hare far away.

'How do you feel about leaving, Charlie?' murmured Rose. 'I must admit I'm a bit sad. I know it hasn't been easy for you, but I feel good knowing that we faced a big challenge and succeeded. Even though we're all going back to the suburbs, we know that we could do it again if we had to.'

'Yes, I'm sure we could,' Charlie said. 'I have enjoyed it and we've learnt a lot . . . but we have our new family to think about now.' He allowed his gaze to wander over the shining landscape, breathing the pure air and listening to the gentle night sounds. An occasional plop of snow sounded, as it fell from a twig on the nearby snow gums. 'I know we'll miss it, but I'm sure we'll come back here often.'

Rose had rested her chin on her paws while he spoke, and gone to sleep. Looking at her lovingly, he thought how much easier it would be for her with the pups back home where they lived.

He spent much of that night re-living their adventures of the past months. Though he did not know it, three silent companions sat close by. They sensed his mixture of sadness and relief. Eventually he too put his chin on his paws, and with a deep groan relaxed into sleep.

The puppies woke at first light and their yelps of 'Where's breakfast?' soon had everyone else awake. The Waters knew that an early start was essential with the puppies if they were to get back to the vehicle in two days. Over breakfast the family discussed a visit to the vet as soon as they got home.

'The pups will have a natural immunity through Rose's milk, but they must be ten or eleven weeks old now. We must get them to the vet straight away,' said Mr Waters.

They sat eating in silence for a few minutes and then Mrs Waters, who had been thinking about this for some time, said, 'What do we do with the pups when we're home? Four is a lot, I know, but I couldn't bear to split them up or take them away from Rose. What do you think, darling?'

'Oh, Dad! Of course we can't!' cried the children in unison, and then Kate added, 'We've got a big block and plenty of room for them to run and play. Mummy's right, Rose would be heartbroken if she lost the puppies now.'

Mr Waters thought for a little while, looking at the happy parents with their fluffy family. 'You're right of course, all three of you. We couldn't even think of splitting them up, so you children had better start thinking of names.'

Everyone laughed happily, and the children hugged all the dogs in turn.

'Come on now,' he said. 'We must get packed up and be on our way. I'm not sure where we'll be tonight with four small pups. They shouldn't overdo it, so we'll need to stop often, and we may need to carry them a bit. Fortunately there's plenty of water on the way.'

Soon they had everything together in their backpacks, and they all walked to the stream for a final deep drink. Then slowly they set off up towards the rim of the valley. As they paused by the snow gums at the top, Charlie and Rose looked back down to the rocky outcrop and the cave which had been their home for nearly six months. They looked at one another and smiled, then turned to follow the family as they made their way down

'Look at him go ... he runs like the wind ...'

towards a broad snow plain. The puppies romped and rolled down the slope, happy in this new adventure.

They soon came to another creek and had a second drink. The puppies then set off back the way they'd come.

'No, this way, children,' called Rose, 'we're going home.'

Puzzled but obedient, they turned and raced after the Waters family, the smallest male way out in front.

'Look at him go!' said Peter. 'He runs like the wind.'

'So he does,' said Kate, and then they looked at each other. 'Let's call him Wind, Peter, he'll always be the fastest.' And so the first name was given.

Full of feminine wiles, the smaller of the two girls compensated for her lesser speed by nipping at feet and pulling on tails, and when everyone stopped for a rest she insisted on more activity, especially chewing on her father's ears.

As usual he tolerated it for a while, then his deep growl indicated enough.

So off she went to bother one of the other pups.

'She's an active little tyke,' said Mr Waters. 'I wonder if she ever stops. She might have been born during a storm, because she's certainly whipping one up here!'

It was Mrs Waters' turn to give the name, Storm, to the little bundle of energy.

Aaron, Emma and Airlie had decided to accompany the group for a little way, and they enjoyed the loving conversations that took place about naming the pups.

What an extraordinary coincidence that they were the very same names that Charlie and Rose had given them. What would they do for the bigger boy and girl? Surely they couldn't possibly pick the same names for all four.

'Well, Kate,' said Mr Waters. 'You're so clever with names, what about the other two, the bigger ones?'

'They're so gentle, Dad, and they seem very wise for little puppies. I've been thinking of that nursery we used to visit. You remember, they had those two Airedales? That's why we got Charlie and Rose, we liked those two so much. And do you remember the people who had the nursery always said that when they died, they came to live up here in their spirit place. Do you think we could call the puppies after them and pretend that the spirits have been reborn in these two?'

'Of course we can, what a lovely idea,' said Mrs Waters, 'What were their names again?'

'The boy was Aaron and the girl was Emma,' said Kate.

And looking at this sturdy determined pair pushing through a field of daisies, all the family thought just how right these names were.

Aaron and Emma stopped in their tracks. 'I find this hard to believe, Aaron,' Emma said with wonderment. 'But however it's happened, I'm so happy.'

'Well, we may never know, Emma,' replied Aaron, 'but like you, I'm very pleased.' He looked quite astonished. Airlie twinkled her eyes at him. She thought it was pretty good, too.

THREE FRIENDS

So the three companions stopped, and turned back to sit on the rim of their valley. They gazed after the receding figures, listening to the voices becoming fainter in the clear air. They saw Charlie and Rose stop and look back and then move on again, and they could no longer hear any sounds but for a light wind, and a currawong calling from far off.

Now the figures were very small, but Aaron was sure that he saw Charlie stop and look back one last time, before they all disappeared behind a rocky outcrop covered in stunted snow gums.

None of them spoke, just enjoyed the silence as they sat together. Airlie turned her head to sniff the fragrance of the late wild flowers wafting to them on the breeze.

She broke the silence. ‘Well, I — I — suppose I should go too, now that they’ve gone. I’ve had a wonderful time over the months I’ve been here, but I should be going.’

None of them spoke, just enjoyed the silence as they sat together ...

Aaron and Emma exchanged glances.

'Oh, there's no rush, Airlie,' said Aaron. 'Unless you really feel you have to go. We still have lots to show you, and even Emma and I haven't seen the hut that Charlie found.'

Airlie's heart missed a beat. She loved them both so much, but she didn't want to impose on their lives. Her eyes misted over.

'I really shouldn't stay any longer, the heavy snows will be coming soon, and I need to find my cave again before it starts.' Her voice was very soft.

'Won't you be lonely?' Emma asked.

'Oh, I've done all right all these years; I'm fine.' She spoke bravely, but they could tell that she was not saying this with much conviction.

There was a long pause, then Aaron spoke.

'Emma and I have talked about this a lot, Airlie, and we feel that — but only if it's all right by you — that you were so close to Bill, and we were the same to Sue and Bill — that we really would like you to stay with us from now on. Three can live as happily as two, and besides, we've still got years of stories to tell. What do you say, will you live with us?'

Airlie was overwhelmed. All the dreams and hopes she had built up over the past weeks suddenly came true with Aaron's words.

'Of course I would love to stay, nothing would give me greater joy. You are such a generous and loving brother and sister for me, and I will never leave you, until the vapours of eternity call.' Her voice trembled with happiness.

And so they sat in silence, not touching, but forever close. And the light wind brought new perfumes to their nostrils, and their eyes followed a flock of black cockatoos on their journey to the lowlands.

Their spirits were one.

EPILOGUE
LITTLE MEGGY BEAR

Sometimes the three of them wandered afar together. At other times, Airlie would go off on her own. 'It's not that I don't want to be with you both all the time, but you've got your memories to talk over, and I've got mine to think about,' she would say.

She might be gone for a few hours or a few days. When she came back, they were all pleased to see each other. 'What have you seen?' and 'Where did you go?' they asked each other immediately. And as the seasons passed, their patterns developed.

It was during such a separation in early spring one year that Aaron and Emma were enjoying scouting about the snow-free ground for new wild flowers. A movement in the distance caught Aaron's eye.

'Here's Airlie back from her journey, Emma . . . she seems to be stopping every few paces and looking around.' Emma followed his gaze. 'Yes, she is acting strangely . . . perhaps it's a hare that she's flushed out of the heath.'

They watched the lone figure's slow progress. Suddenly she stopped still and gazed in their direction. 'Airlie . . . what's wrong?' called Aaron. 'Why don't you come to us?'

The figure hesitated for a few moments, then began walking towards them again. She did not take her eyes off them. When she was within thirty metres or so, Aaron realised his mistake.

'Emma, it's not Airlie. It's another Airedale. Wherever would she have come from?'

'Well, that I don't know, but I'm sure she's looking for us. We must make her welcome.'

'Of course, where are my manners?' said Aaron. 'Hullo there, can we help you? Are you looking for someone in particular?'

Emma looked at him disapprovingly. 'That's a bit formal; make her really welcome.'

Before he could respond, the new Airedale, now only a few metres away, spoke.

'I hope I'm not intruding, but I'm new here, and I was looking for three Airedales,' she said shyly, looking around.

'Oh, there usually are three of us,' said

'I hope I'm not intruding, but I'm new here ...'

Aaron. 'Airlie's just gone off for a little bit; she'll be back soon.'

There was a slight hesitation from the new little girl, but there was a brighter light in her eyes. 'Did you say Airlie?'

'Yes,' said Emma.

'Then you must be Aaron and Emma,' she said more confidently.

'We are,' they said together. 'But how did you know?'

'The white swallow told me. It was the one who guided me up to the high wild country. It said I would find you.'

'Well I never,' exclaimed Aaron. 'But what made you want to come here in the first place?'

'My family knows your Sue and Bill, and they were always talking about where your spirits had gone.'

As the three had been speaking, Airlie arrived back from her journey. She sat beside Emma and listened to the new arrival's story.

'They didn't know about Airlie being here,' the new girl said. 'It was the white swallow who told me about her on my journey here.'

'What's your name?' asked Airlie gently.

'I was called Meg at first, but then everyone called me Meggy Bear. I suppose it was because I'm so woolly, and I love being cuddled.'

Don't we all, the other three thought to themselves. Each had a memory of strong arms holding them tightly, of lots of kisses being dropped on nose and eyes, and in Aaron's case, a favourite babyhood recollection of having his tummy blown and blurted upon.

'Well, if your family knows ours,' Aaron asked, 'who are they?'

'You remember Marney? She and your Sue and Bill work together sometimes, something to do with nurseries and plants. Marney always loved you and Emma and Alice, and asked Sue and Bill to help her find an Airedale, and that's when I became part of the family.'

'Now I understand,' said Aaron. 'But wasn't that just a few seasons ago? You'll forgive me for being so rude, but aren't you very young?'

'Yes, I must be,' Meg replied, and then added with sadness, 'I didn't seem to be with the family for very long at all. I do miss them; they all loved me, and I couldn't have been happier. I loved them so much, specially Marney. She took me everywhere with her, and she always talked to me lots.'

There was a silence in which all of them thought of the happy times and the missed families.

'Well,' said Emma, breaking the silence. 'I think it will be nice to have someone young to keep us oldies on our toes. And we'll look after you always. And don't forget, one day you will be together with all your family. That's the way things are here. It just takes a bit of time. But in the meantime, there's lots of things to do and see and learn, and soon you'll love it as much as we do.'

She knew Meggy Bear was feeling sad and lost, and she leaned forward and gave her a touch on the nose. 'You'll see. We'll be your family, and we'll all be together.'

Together, they rose and began moving across the snow-patched plain.

Aaron and Emma were slightly ahead, with Airlie shoulder to shoulder with Meggy Bear, as she began to familiarise her with her new world.

'We're becoming quite a family, aren't we, Em?' said Aaron.

She simply nodded wisely.

And so another eternal journey of the spirit began. In years to come, it would be Meggy Bear who would welcome newly arrived and uncertain spirits to the magical forever country of the high wild plains.

Together, they rose and began moving across the snow-patched plain ...